D0718068

Moving On

By the Same Author

The Kid

Moving On

KEVIN LEWIS

MICHAEL JOSEPH
an imprint of
PENGUIN BOOKS

MICHAEL JOSEPH

Published by the Penguin Group

Penguin Books Ltd, 80 Strand, London WC2R ORL, England

Penguin Group (USA) Inc., 375 Hudson Street, New York, New York 10014, USA

Penguin Group (Canada), 10 Alcorn Avenue, Toronto, Ontario, Canada M4V 3B2

(a division of Pearson Penguin Canada Inc.)

Penguin Ireland, 25 St Stephen's Green, Dublin 2, Ireland

(a division of Penguin Books Ltd)

Penguin Group (Australia), 250 Camberwell Road,

Camberwell, Victoria 3124, Australia (a division of Pearson Australia Group Pty Ltd)

Penguin Books India Pvt Ltd, 11 Community Centre,

Panchsheel Park, New Delhi – 110 017, India

Penguin Group (NZ), cnr Airborne and Rosedale Roads, Albany,

Auckland 1310, New Zealand (a division of Pearson New Zealand Ltd)

Penguin Books (South Africa) (Pty) Ltd, 24 Sturdee Avenue,

Rosebank 2196, South Africa

Penguin Books Ltd, Registered Offices: 80 Strand, London WC2R ORL, England

www.penguin.com

First published 2005

2

Copyright © Kevin Lewis, 2005

The moral right of the author has been asserted

All rights reserved.

Without limiting the rights under copyright
reserved above, no part of this publication may be
reproduced, stored in or introduced into a retrieval system,
or transmitted, in any form or by any means (electronic, mechanical,
photocopying, recording or otherwise), without the prior
written permission of both the copyright owner and
the above publisher of this book

Set in 13.75/16.25 pt Monotype Dante
Typeset by Rowland Phototypesetting Ltd, Bury St Edmunds, Suffolk
Printed in England by Clays Ltd, St Ives plc

A CIP catalogue record for this book is available from the British Library

ISBN 0-718-14742-1
TRADE PAPERBACK ISBN 0-718-14818-5

To the three people who mean
the world to me, Jackie, Charlotte and Nathan

I would like to give a special thank you to Barbara Levy for her honesty and understanding. To my editor Clare Ledingham and the rest of the team at Michael Joseph and Penguin, thank you for your continued support.

Preface

One of the reasons I wrote *The Kid* was to try to exorcize my past. I believed that if I wrote it all down and shared it with my wife, Jackie, I would be able to face the demons that lurked inside my head, clear out all the stuff that I had been suppressing for so long, and we could get on with our lives together.

But I was to have no idea how difficult it would be to deal with and accept the memories that came bubbling to the surface during the writing process. Nor did I have any idea how hard it would be to relive the story over and over again for the press and television, and to suddenly find the eyes of the world upon me. Imagine going out into the street each day and feeling that everyone else knows all your most shameful secrets, while you don't even know their names.

All the time, however, I was able to console myself with the thought that by writing about the past I would be able to make the future better – for us as a family and perhaps even for other people reading the book. So when I discovered that history was repeating itself in the Lewis family, and that Gloria was still behaving towards children in the same way she had behaved towards me, I was at first devastated, then angry and ashamed, and finally determined to do something about it.

But at the same time as dealing with all these over-powering emotions, I was having a ball. Writing a book that was a bestseller was like the icing on the cake of our happy family life. I suddenly had the ability to make my dreams come true. The question was, what were my real dreams? And was that all they were, or could they be turned into reality? As life always shows, nothing is ever as easy as you think.

I

Telling Jackie

The manuscript of *The Kid* was finally ready, but I was apprehensive about giving it to Jackie to read, even though that was the main reason I had written it. Writing an honest account of my life had been a deeply personal and upsetting experience, and there were bits of the story that had proved to be almost unbearably emotional for me to write down and relive. The thought of now showing the manuscript to someone else, even my wife, was making me anxious to say the least. Once she knew the truth there would be no going back. I had heard the phrase 'baring one's soul' but I had never realized how difficult that would be. Now that everything was on paper I must admit I felt naked and vulnerable, and I was nervous about the emotions that were awakening inside me. Seeing my past laid out so vividly in black and white made it harder to deal with.

I wasn't sure how Jackie would react to some of the things that I had revealed. In the process of telling my story I'd found I was stirring up feelings I hadn't experienced before. I suppose that was why I'd been so careful never to think about them. I'd been telling myself that I didn't need to think about the past because dwelling on it wouldn't help me or my family, now or in the future.

Some of the memories I believe I had deliberately avoided experiencing for fear that I wouldn't be able to cope with them. And some of the revelations from my childhood were just plain embarrassing to admit to myself, let alone Jackie: things like wetting the bed and living in a room where the walls were smeared with excrement.

So many of the memories had been locked away for so many years because I'd never wanted to think about them, never wanted to look back at painful, unhappy times. I always preferred looking to the future, making plans and getting on with life in order to escape as far away from my past as possible. I wanted to spend my time thinking about things that I might be able to enjoy, rather than things that I could no longer do anything about. It was as though my subconscious knew those memories would hold me back in the past and so had hidden them away deep inside my head. I've always told myself there is nothing you can do to change the past; what's done is done. But now those memories had resurfaced with the birth of my children and the sight of them growing up brought it all to the front of my mind. This was another reason why I had decided to put it on paper in an attempt to make sense of it all.

Jackie has always accepted me for who I am today and never worried about what might have happened in the past, but I felt I owed it to her to explain why I am the way I am. I wanted her to know everything about me, including things that I would have been unable to find the words to say out loud to her. It was easier just to write it all down and hand it to her. That way I could explain it to her without sounding as if I was feeling sorry for myself. Self-pity is an emotion I firmly believe to be a sign of weakness and something I am always keen to avoid.

The urge to explain things about my past had been becoming stronger as I saw my son growing up and found myself unable to resist thinking about my own childhood when I was his age. Flashbacks to scenes that I had succeeded in putting out of my mind for years had resurfaced as I watched him develop as a child. I did have some flashbacks before he was born and as my daughter was growing up, but they tended to be memories of my sisters and of some of the things that had happened to them and my self-doubts concerning being a father. They were troubling thoughts and hard to ignore, and I believed that writing them down would help me to clear them from my mind, so I wouldn't have to think about them again. It was a bit like preparing a 'things to do' list; once I'd committed my memories to paper I hoped I wouldn't have to remember them any more and would be able to move on and think about other things, good things about my life, my family and my career, knowing that the past was safely recorded somewhere else, somewhere outside my head. Finally my whole life was in the manuscript as I watched it emerge from the printer, the ink still wet, the pages warm and pristine.

The reason I'd decided to write my life story in the first place was because I had made a promise to Jackie a few years before that one day I would explain my past. I knew so much about the person I love, but she knew very little about where I came from. I also wanted her to know everything that had happened to me in the years before I met her, so that she could understand better what was going on in my head as an adult. I'd poured my whole heart into the manuscript, dredging up memories that had been buried for years, to make sure everything was explained and I believed that by doing this I might be able to get it out of my head once and for all and move on.

There were parts of the book that I found very hard to write, and I found myself feeling confused as each door in my memory led to another and then another; taking me on a journey deeper and deeper into my past; uncovering horrors I had wanted to forget. I had very few happy memories before I met Jackie but it was no good pretending my life had started on the day she came into my life.

It was when trying to tackle these emotional scenes from my childhood and adolescence that I realized I needed help from someone who could look at the story in a clear and objective way. I decided to enlist the help of Andrew, a writer. We worked together on the most difficult parts, breaking them down one by one and then placing them in chronological order to ensure they made complete sense by the time Jackie came to read them.

She'd known all along that I was writing it, and that it was going to be about my life before I met her, but she didn't pester me to let her read it. Every so often she would ask how it was going and I would reply 'nearly there', and she would just smile encouragingly.

Once the manuscript was finished and ready for Jackie, Andrew said he thought it read very well and asked if I'd ever considered showing it to a literary agent or a publisher with a view to having it published.

'No,' was my instant reply. At that stage there was no

way I could even contemplate seeing my life published as a book. It was going to be hard enough to reveal my past to Jackie, let alone to someone I had never met. Andrew saw I wasn't ready and so didn't push the matter any further, apart from saying that if I did change my mind he knew a literary agent by the name of Barbara Levy who might want to take a look at it. Not knowing anything about the publishing industry, the name meant nothing to me, and I put the whole idea out of my head. Anyway, I told myself, Jackie hadn't read it yet and I wanted her reaction to the material before I even thought about showing it to anyone else. I needed her approval and to know that she would still see me as the normal bubbly person I had been since meeting her.

Jackie knows I've never been good at showing my emotions except with my children and has never tried to force me to explain or ask me difficult questions, which is just one of the hundreds of reasons why I love her as much as I do. She instinctively knew there was something very wrong in my relationship with my parents because of the lack of communication between us, but she didn't pry as to why that might be.

On the odd occasions when Gloria, my mother, would ring I would know instantly who it was through her distinct loud tones and I would hand the phone straight to Jackie, with no explanation and barely a hello to Gloria. Jackie would handle the conversation politely and discreetly, never questioning me afterwards as to why I might not want to speak to my own mother. As far as I know Gloria never wanted to talk to me on these calls anyway, apparently relieved when I passed her straight to Jackie. If Jackie picked up the phone first she would whisper who it was and I would shake my head, not wanting to talk to her. I don't think Gloria believed I remembered any of my childhood. Maybe she had forgotten most of it herself or chose not to remember. Gloria would then talk to Jackie as though everything was fine between me and Gloria, and that we had a caring, normal mother and son relationship. Sometimes I wanted to grab the phone and say, 'Stop pretending you've been this wonderful mother. You're so full of self-pity, don't you see what you've done?' But if I did that I'd have had to reveal my past.

I hadn't wanted to give the manuscript to Jackie until I was sure it was as good as it could be, but once it was ready I still sat on it for around a week. I would keep looking at it neatly stacked on the shelf waiting for the right moment, until one evening I thought 'what the hell', picked it up and walked into the kitchen where Jackie was busy clearing up for the night. She saw me coming in, manuscript held tightly under my arm. We looked at each other, and she immediately saw what I was holding and gave me a reassuring look.

'Here it is,' I said, placing it on the work surface then walking off quickly before she could say anything. There it lay – my whole life on a hundred pages of neatly printed white paper. It didn't look much, but it was my story. Some bits I was proud of, like helping Chris in the frozen lake and Kimberley in Yarborough – and later standing up for myself and saving the house from repossession. But it also contained my secrets. I had no idea how she was going to react to what she was about to read, especially my detailed account of my indiscretion with another woman. So many times I had put it in then taken it back out again. Eventually I thought it best to leave it in because I felt if I'd left it out, she might sense I wasn't being completely honest with her, and it was very important to me to tell her the truth. I owed it to Jackie, so she might understand me better.

Because it was late and Jackie was tired she didn't read it that night. She tucked it away in a drawer just in case the children saw it as she knew that would lead to one hundred and one questions that neither of us were prepared to answer. It was the following evening, once the children had had their bedtime stories and were fast asleep, that she picked up the manuscript and brought it into the lounge. I was sprawled out on the sofa watching television and, as we exchanged smiles, I saw the pages in her hand. I realized she was ready to settle down to read it, and I knew I couldn't be in the same room as her.

'I'm just going to get some petrol for the car,' I said, clambering off the sofa.

I'm sure she knew it was an excuse and that I just wanted to be out of the way. But she seemed less taken aback by my leaving than that I willingly handed her the remote control! As I went out of the room I saw her switch off the television, swing her legs up on to the sofa and open the first page. The house was silent and there was an air of anticipation and an atmosphere I can't describe. I got the car keys and quietly closed the door behind me. I drove to the petrol station, filled up and then drove around the countryside for at least an hour and a half, singing along to the music on the car stereo, trying to imagine what Jackie might be thinking as she discovered who her husband truly was and what had really happened to him. I drove until I was tired of the music and my eyes felt heavy. When I got back home I walked round to the front door and I saw the lamp in the lounge was still on and, through the window, Jackie sitting frozen on the sofa – it was as though she hadn't moved in all the time I had been out. I quietly opened the front door, kicked my trainers off and popped my head round the door. The first thing I noticed was the manuscript lying open on the coffee table. As my eyes focused in the dimly lit room I saw my wife, her eyes red and blotchy. The television was still switched off and she seemed to be a hundred miles away. It was obvious she was upset, but when our eyes met neither of us knew what to say to each other. I didn't want to talk about it or hug her, for fear of the emotions that would be unleashed. She looked stunned and neither of us knew what to do. So I thought it best to leave it and pretend nothing out of the ordinary was going on. I took a deep breath and smiled.

'Hi,' I said, cheerfully. 'I'm going up to bed.'

She looked up at me with a sweet, strained smile.

'Cheer up,' I said, 'it's not that bad.' I didn't know what else to say.

She smiled again, but the effort seemed even harder for her and I saw her bottom lip shaking. I went upstairs and got ready for bed.

It took Jackie a long time to come upstairs that evening. As I lay awake in bed she stayed downstairs on the sofa, lost in her own thoughts. I really wanted to go back down, put my arms around her and comfort her, but I think she just wanted to be alone, too stunned and angry to know how to react. When she eventually came up it took us ages to go to sleep. Neither of us knew what to say to each other, and so again we didn't say anything. At first we lay back to back. I knew she was upset and so I made the first move by touching her leg with my foot and stroking it gently. She stroked back with her other leg on mine and I rolled on to my back. Jackie rolled on to hers and then turned and rested her head on my chest. I put my arm lovingly around her. I felt a warm tear fall on to my chest and I hugged her tightly, comforting her until she finally fell asleep.

For the next few evenings, after we'd put the children to bed, she would sit down with the manuscript and take in a few more chapters. I still couldn't stay in the same room while she was reading because every so often she would glance up at me and I couldn't bear to look her in the face, so I would find myself something else to do in another part of the house, or I would go out on some fictitious errand or other. Actually, I told myself, this is a bloody good time to sort out the garage.

I think she knew what was going on and also I think she wanted to be left alone to absorb everything without having to worry about my feelings. We didn't speak about the manuscript at all while she was reading; we just carried on with life as normal, as if nothing out of the ordinary was happening. It was a bit quieter than usual around the house, but the kids always made sure that didn't last for long. Being observant of their parents' moods, like most children, they sometimes asked if anything was wrong, especially with Mummy. We would both just smile and carry on having fun and enjoying family life in what was generally a very happy home. As Jackie was coming to the end of the book I noticed she was becoming a lot more cheerful and back to her usual self. I wondered what she would say and how she would behave towards me now that she knew so much.

Finally the silence about the book that had hung between us throughout those one hundred pages was broken. She came out to the dining room where I was sitting late one evening, trying to keep busy. Putting the manuscript down at one end of the table, she walked up behind me and wrapped her arms tightly around me.

'Everything makes sense now,' she said. 'I'm so proud of you.'

'Are you all right with it?' I asked, my hand holding hers.

'Kevin,' she replied, 'I married you for who you are now, no matter what happened in the past.'

We smiled at each other and I realized I'd done the right thing; she now knew who I was before we met. Showing her so much of myself had brought us even closer together than we were before. She could understand so many things that must have puzzled her about the way I behaved sometimes; how I was so ambitious and determined to succeed and the way I sometimes became over-protective of the children, and how I would jump in to help my brothers and sisters at a moment's notice. She would understand why I didn't let the children see their grandparents and so many other decisions that must have seemed puzzling in the past.

'It's all behind me now,' I said. 'I don't want to dwell on it any more. I want us to get on with our lives together and look to the future.' I knew she understood and that she wouldn't be referring to any of the incidents she'd read about again unless I brought the subject up first, which I had no intention of doing.

She just smiled. 'Don't forget to enjoy now,' she said and kissed me on the cheek. I knew she was right. It would be all too easy to become so wrapped up in the future that I let the present slip past.

'I'm never going to talk to Gloria or Dennis again,' she said, looking down at the table.

I stood up and we held on to each other tightly for ages before going into the lounge to watch some television together. We began to play and joke about who should have the remote control and then something funny came on and it wasn't long before we were laughing again.

Later that evening I told her what Andrew had said about showing the book to an agent, and that I wasn't sure about letting other people look at it because it was so personal, and because I wasn't certain whether there would be any legal comeback for any of the misdemeanours I'd admitted to. We talked about it and eventually agreed there was no harm in at least showing it to this agent to see what she thought. It might be that she wouldn't think it was good enough to publish anyway and that would be the end of it. It could then be boxed up and put away for ever. If she did like it we could cross that bridge when we came to it. I called Andrew the next day and told him to let the agent, Barbara Levy, take a look at it.

2

Finding an Agent

During the writing process, especially at the beginning when I was thinking about my early years, old childhood habits had started to surface and I couldn't shake them off, even after the manuscript was finished. It was as if stirring up the mud at the bottom of my memory had allowed these long-buried habits to float to the surface from their hiding places in my subconscious. Jackie noticed that I wasn't as cheerful and bubbly as usual. I seemed to be stuck in my own quiet world and incapable of spending much time in any one room, feeling that I had to keep moving around. She kept asking me if I was all right.

'I'm fine,' I would say with an exaggerated grin, not sure whether I was or not. She asked me so often that it began to annoy me.

I also started to become anxious very easily and when this happened I would stand in a certain way, my right hand rubbing nervously down my leg, shuffling my feet, as I did as a child when I was about to be attacked. My eating habits and table manners started to change. At the dinner table I would clean my cutlery obsessively, licking it and then furiously rubbing it on my clothing until it gleamed in the light. It was already sparkly clean but that didn't make any difference. During each meal I would repeatedly brush the tablecloth with my hands, desperate for any crumbs to be wiped away leaving everything clean. If we went out to dinner, as soon as I finished a course I would hold up my plate for it to be collected by the waiter or move it away from me to the other side of the table. I'd wipe the tablecloth clean of breadcrumbs with my serviette, and only then feel able to rest happily and watch Jackie eat.

I was eating faster and faster, stuffing food into my mouth and sometimes swallowing without even chewing, then placing my hand over my mouth so no one could see what I was doing. As a child I had always covered my mouth after cramming as much as I could into it in order to stop it being taken out again, or just to hide the fact that I was eating at all. It was happening again and I would finish my meal before Jackie and the kids had even taken their third mouthful. I also took to sniffing everything, like a suspicious dog, whether it was my food or my clothes or just passing scents in the air. I was becoming more and more aware of the world around me; sights and sounds as well as smells, just as I had been as a child. Some smells reminded me vividly of my past: the smell of freshly polished wooden floors would take me back to the many schools I was sent to that I never fitted in at; or the smell of the rubbish as I emptied the bins would remind me of the tin house and the house in Norbury which we moved to later on. But there were also good smells – I always found taking in deep breaths of fresh air and the scent of flowers uplifting and it made me feel happy. So to overcome the problem of the smells I took to buying Jackie fresh flowers regularly. I loved the fact it brought a smile to her face, especially because I wasn't doing it to apologize for something.

My sleeping became even lighter than usual; the slightest movement from the children's rooms would have me leaping out of bed to check they were OK. When I got to their bedrooms there they would be, sleeping peacefully, and I would return to bed, ready to listen again. Any night-time sounds made me tense, whether it was the children mumbling in their dreams, air bubbles whispering through the heating system or the boiler sparking into life. The nights were becoming long and tiring.

The children noticed that I was becoming more withdrawn and this made me feel even worse about what I had written, frustrated that I couldn't get back to my cheerful self. I'd always enjoyed a glass of red wine and I began drinking more. This started when I began the book and soon I was consuming a bottle a night.

Worst of all, I could hear myself saying 'sorry' the whole time; sorry for this, sorry for that, sometimes sorry for the sake of saying sorry. I was really starting to annoy myself. It got to the point where the children started doing the same, apologizing for no reason, and it sounded terrible to me. It was obvious where they were catching the habit from.

'Never say sorry unless you've done something wrong and you mean it. Don't just say it for the sake of it,' I told them sternly, although I was speaking to myself as much as to them. Discovering I was behaving like this shook me. I realized I had to look at what was happening to me.

It was then, as I stood outside myself and watched the way in which I had been behaving lately, that I worked out what was happening. I had locked my past away so tightly for so long, never wanting or needing to deal with it, that now I had written it down it was like opening a can of particularly poisonous worms, allowing the imprisoned memories to burst out of their hiding places. I was also beginning to feel emotions I had never experienced before – emotions I had always studiously avoided feeling – and now I had opened up that can of worms I didn't know how to deal with the issues I was facing. Or how to keep them from overwhelming me and more importantly my family.

I'd written the book in order to release myself from the past, but it seemed to have made things worse; this wasn't supposed to happen, I kept telling myself over and over again. I found that I got emotional every time I thought about anything to do with my childhood. Mental pictures were coming back with shocking clarity. I could vividly see the room that I was forced to spend so much time in, even smell it sometimes. I could visualize clearly my childish scribbles on the filthy walls. These scribbles depicted a life outside the house, and had helped me escape from the reality of what was going on all around me; but they were cries for help that no one would see until it was too late to do anything.

By facing up to my past I had removed the mental barriers I'd erected over the years and had released the floodgates; and I had no idea how to handle these difficult emotions. I was in danger of drowning and was clinging to my bad habits like liferafts, or like a small child might cling to a comforter or sucking their thumb.

A few days later Andrew heard back from Barbara that she liked what she had read and wanted to meet me face to face. It was arranged that I would go to see her at her office in London a few days later. This was good news as far as the book went, but unnerving news for me. I was afraid the unfamiliar emotions that were welling up inside were going to overwhelm me and make the meeting difficult. In business meetings I could always be strong and hold my own because there was nothing personal involved. It was just a transaction between two companies. But this was different. This was all about me and my life. It was a different kind of meeting and I didn't know how to handle it. The more I thought about what might happen when this unknown woman began asking me intimate questions about my past, the more apprehensive I became.

The night before I was due to go I was unable to sleep, tossing and turning all night, wondering how this stranger would react to me and how I would react to her. During those long hours of darkness I thought about everything I'd written. Was I just feeling sorry for myself? Or had I never accepted my past for what it was? This manuscript was supposed to release me from my past so I could move on, but it was making things worse. Had it all been a terrible mistake? I didn't feel how I had expected to feel. If I had known it was going to be like this I would never have written it down on paper in the first place. But I had written it, and now I was being offered some choices as to what I might do. It would be foolish not to at least listen to the possibilities open to me.

This unknown woman I was going to meet was the only person in the world who'd read the manuscript apart from Jackie and Andrew. She was the first stranger who would know all about my past before even meeting me. She would know about the things that had been done to me and the things I had done to other people. Almost all my secrets had been laid bare and I felt sure she would be judging me as a result.

She'd already said she liked the book, which was good, and meant I didn't have to worry about retelling the story to her, or about convincing her that it would make a good book; but how would I behave with her and what questions would she ask me? Would I be able to control the emotions, which felt so new and raw, when I talked about my past to her? She was bound to ask me questions about the difficult times. I didn't want her to feel sorry for me; that was the last thing I had ever wanted. I never wanted pity when I was a child and I certainly didn't want it now. I thought other people's pity was insulting, and would always hold me back. Only the weak, I believed, feel sorry for themselves. But I knew at the same time I had to get control of all these new emotions if I was going to find any mental tranquillity again.

I got up early the next morning, bored of lying in bed, my brain wide awake but my eyes feeling heavy from lack of sleep, and set off for London. I didn't put any music on during the trip; I wanted it to be quiet so I could reflect on all the thoughts I'd had the night before.

I reached the offices three quarters of an hour early for the appointment. I preferred it that way. The last thing I wanted was to be arriving late and flustered. I needed to have time to gather my thoughts. I parked the car and sat, composing myself. As the minutes ticked past agonizingly slowly, I tried to picture what would be happening over the following hour or two. It was as if I was in a trance, thinking about what would happen next, working on automatic pilot. My head was hurting from all the questions that were circling around it, finding answers to none of them. In the end I clapped my hands together as if to snap myself out of my thoughts.

'Just keep cool,' I reassured my reflection in the rear-view mirror. I turned on the car stereo as a distraction, playing some Red Hot Chilli Peppers and Marilyn Manson, laughing at my own foolishness as I tried to sing along.

When the moment to go in finally arrived I made my way to her office with my rucksack on my back. It contained the green file with all the evidence from Social Services to prove my story in case Barbara challenged it, and the big black sketchbook that I use for all my ideas and inventions. I rang the bell and was buzzed into the impressive-looking building. Her secretary greeted me with a friendly smile and led me into a small reception area. She offered me a seat while we waited for Barbara to finish whatever she was doing, but I chose to stand, not yet ready to settle.

My eyes scanned over the massive bookshelf that covered one whole wall, studying row upon row of books. It was peaceful inside the office, comfortably furnished, and a thousand miles from the traffic and bustle of the streets outside. It was a calm environment and I immediately began to feel less intimidated. I had seen a closed door as I came in and guessed that the woman I was coming to meet, the woman who knew everything about me, was sitting behind it.

'Are these all clients of the agency?' I asked, trying to break the silence that very quickly settled between us.

'Yes,' the receptionist smiled encouragingly, 'they're all Barbara's clients.'

As I got to the end of the rows I heard the door to the other office open and I turned round. Suddenly Barbara was there, an elegant woman with a voice so calm and soft it took me by surprise. Never having been used to soft voices in my childhood, they have a particularly soothing effect on me. Jackie has the same air of tranquillity about her, which is one of the reasons I fell in love with her.

'Kevin, hi, I'm Barbara,' she said as I put out my hand and she shook it gently. I returned her smile with my head down.

She led me through to her office, which was pleasantly furnished with yet more bookcases filled with neatly aligned books. She invited me to sit on the sofa, and offered me a drink.

'Water, please,' I replied, my voice a little hesitant.

As she went to fetch it my eyes wandered along the lines of books and over the manuscripts, which were on the floor in piles. It was a very comfortable room, everything neat and tidy and in its place, with a vase of fresh flowers on the table. The room smelled less like an office and more like a home. Barbara was back with my glass of water and offered to take my jacket.

'No thank you,' I said abruptly.

She must have seen that I looked nervous and uncomfortable as she calmly sat on a chair opposite me. If I'd had butterflies before, they were now doubling their efforts to escape from inside my stomach.

'I thoroughly enjoyed reading the book,' she said. 'Has Jackie read it?'

'Yes.'

'What does she think about you coming here today?'

'She's fine with it,' I said, keeping my answers controlled and to the point in case I got tongue-tied.

My palms were sweaty as I clenched and unclenched my fingers, and I began nervously rubbing my hand up and down my leg. My discomfort must have been obvious because she kept the meeting short and to the point, which I appreciated greatly. As this lady tried to put me at my ease I could feel tears welling up inside me even before I started to talk. I wasn't sure I was going to be able to get the words out and so I remained quiet and listened to what she had to say. 'Don't get upset,' I told myself, 'just keep it together. Don't be a fool.'

She explained how she would go about marketing the book if I was happy to work with her; how she would send the manuscript out to four publishers she thought might be interested and invite them to make offers, and what was likely to happen after that. She was talking about contracts and percentages and I was only really hearing half of what she was saying because my own thoughts and feelings were rushing in so fast.

Fighting back the emotions that threatened to break through, I told her of my reservations about publishing – and how I wasn't sure that I was ready to cope with the world knowing my secrets. The meeting was coming to an end and I was beginning to breathe more easily.

'So where do we go from here?' I asked, as I stood up to leave about an hour after arriving. 'If we decide to go ahead, do I ask you to work for me, or is it the other way round?'

We decided that if I went ahead it would be more a question of working together.

'Cool for cats,' I said, and we both smiled at each other. I was feeling more relaxed now, knowing that the meeting was coming to an end, and I said I would discuss it with Jackie before making a final decision.

I also now felt able to tell her what was on my mind. 'The book is so personal,' I admitted. 'There are parts I'm ashamed of and bits that were only meant for Jackie.'

'Kevin,' she said, gently but firmly, 'you have nothing to be ashamed of.'

I could understand that in her eyes I might not have anything to be ashamed of, but in mine things looked different and I couldn't change the way I felt.

'Kevin,' she went on, 'if you had written it to be published would you have been so forthcoming and truthful about your life?'

Almost certainly not, I thought to myself, but I didn't say anything, simply shaking my head.

We shook hands and as the office door closed behind me I gave a huge sigh of relief; partly relieved because I had managed not to get upset about my past and partly because I hadn't been asked to prove anything. To have to prove to a stranger what had happened, recalling the beatings and tortures all over again and justifying the actions of others was something I couldn't have faced. As I stood outside the door I held my hands out just to see how much they were shaking. I walked towards the stairs and wiped away a tear that had rolled down my cheek. I could see that this was all going to be much harder than I had anticipated.

Even in that initial, brief meeting Barbara had explained a great deal about the industry I was on the verge of being catapulted into. I felt that if I chose to take the plunge I would now have in Barbara an ally I could trust, someone who would always have my interests at heart. At the back of my mind, however, a little warning voice was still telling me not to get too excited, that no one, as I had learned many times before, can be trusted until they have proved themselves to be trustworthy.

That evening, over yet another bottle of wine, Jackie and I talked it through and decided that we would take the plunge and let Barbara try to sell the book. It didn't have to be an absolutely final decision yet, we could always change our minds again later, but we might as well find out if publishers were interested at all. If they weren't then we could forget about the whole thing and get on with the rest of our lives, having lost nothing. I rang Barbara the next day to tell her of our decision and she promised to get back to me as soon as she'd had some reactions from publishers.

3

Feeling Naked

Once Jackie and I had decided that we would see if the book could be published, Barbara sent it to the four publishers she had in mind, telling them that she would like to hear their reactions within a fortnight. I decided to put the whole thing out of my mind, that way I wouldn't be disappointed if no one liked it. If anything came of it, I was sure Barbara would be ringing me very quickly.

In the meantime the flashbacks were coming thick and fast. It seemed endless. When I was alone at home I would sit down and think of the past, seeing myself with my legs up in the air, kicking my own mother just to get her off me, or trying to wriggle away from Dennis while the stick or buckle was coming down on me. I would look down and catch myself anxiously rubbing my legs, as if I was trying to soothe the pain away. The worst thoughts were when I remembered some of the times that I couldn't get away and I would simply bury my head in a cushion and cry. I felt so stupid to be getting upset about something that I never wanted to think about again, but I couldn't seem to stop the memories from surfacing.

Within a week Barbara had called to tell me that three

of the publishers had made offers for roughly the same amount, and that the editorial team at Michael Joseph, one of the publishing houses owned by the Penguin Group, had asked for a meeting with me the following day, a Friday. It felt good that they liked what I'd written, but at the same time I could feel the uncomfortable swirl of emotions that I had experienced when I went to meet Barbara for the first time.

Barbara went to great lengths to explain to me who would be in the room at the meeting and assured me that they were very interested to chat to me. A time was set, just before lunch, and she and I agreed to meet in the company's lobby area before going up to their offices. I was glad when she said she was coming with me as I certainly didn't want to go alone.

When I told Jackie the news, she thought it was great that such well-known publishers should be showing an interest. I knew she was right and the fact that one of them wanted to meet me was even more promising, but it meant I was going to have to put myself through another meeting with strangers who would know everything about my life, including all the most humiliating details.

That night, just like the night before I was first due to meet Barbara, I didn't sleep a single wink. My mind was churning as I wondered how I would behave with these people and what would happen when I got there. I was trying to picture the scene so that I wouldn't be taken completely unawares, but I couldn't imagine what a publisher's office would look like. All evening I'd been trying to hypnotize myself not to get upset when they asked me about incidents in the book, remembering how I'd felt talking to Barbara for the first time. The last thing I wanted to do was to burst into tears in front of a bunch of strangers.

The next morning, after a restless night, my eyes heavy once again and my head aching with all the same questions as before, I headed back up to London. Before leaving I packed my rucksack once more with the green folder from Social Services, just in case they wanted proof that I was telling the truth, and my big black book in case they wanted to see other things I had done. I also packed a notepad, which was something I had always done when I was attending business meetings. I took it so I could make notes if I needed to, but also, more importantly, so I could persuade myself it was a business meeting, thereby making it seem less personal.

Although I knew it was possible that nothing in my life would be the same again after that Friday morning, which was one of the many reasons I was feeling so nervous, I had no idea just how much everything would change as I made my way into London with my rucksack firmly on my shoulders.

It was late morning when Barbara and I met in the lobby of the Penguin headquarters in the Strand and I was relieved to see a familiar face, someone who was comfortable in an environment where I was feeling completely out of my depth. I felt like a little boy again, stepping out into a grown-up world for the first time. It reminded me of an occasion when I was small when I'd dressed as Worzel Gummidge for a school play and walked out on to the stage in front of a silent audience.

Our family was well-known in the neighbourhood and I felt they were just waiting to see how someone from the Lewis family with our reputation would behave. Like then I was unsure what was expected of me. I felt under pressure. I wanted to do my best, but was anxious I'd let myself down.

The lobby was impersonal and the anonymous surroundings gave no clues as to what might lie ahead as we registered our arrival with reception.

'Are you ready, Kevin?' Barbara asked as we sat down to wait.

'Yep,' I replied. She could see I was anxious. Sweat was starting to trickle down the side of my face.

'It will be OK, Kevin. Just be yourself,' she said with a reassuring smile. I took a deep breath and smiled back.

Then with the ping of the lift coming to our floor the doors opened and Lindsey Jordan, an editorial director from Michael Joseph, came down to collect us and take us up to their boardroom. Barbara stood up to greet her. I followed her lead and found myself stepping back behind Barbara, wanting her to do the talking on my behalf. It was as though I was standing behind a teacher as I was introduced to yet another new class. The two women obviously knew one another and greeted each other warmly. For them I guess it was just business as usual. Then Lindsey came round to me.

'You must be Kevin,' she said with a wide, friendly smile. I couldn't find any words so I just shook her proffered hand and smiled back, my throat too tight to speak.

The greetings dealt with, she led us to the lifts and

she and Barbara made small talk as we ascended. They tried to include me in the conversation with polite questions, to which my answers were brief and quiet. I could think of nothing to say as I fought to control the mixture of excitement and panic that was gripping me as we rose further and further from the streets outside, where only a few minutes before I had been just another anonymous person who passers-by knew nothing about. All I could think of was that I wished Jackie was by my side. So that's what I did and, as I turned to look in the lift mirror, there she was, standing beside me behind Barbara and Lindsey, like my own personal genie. A grin spread across my face as I turned to look at her beautiful face and encouraging smile.

Jackie disappeared when the lift doors opened to send us on our journey. As we entered the offices Barbara and Lindsey walked ahead and I followed on behind, gazing around in wide-eyed wonder. The first thing I noticed, and what took me aback, was how quiet it was. It was more like a library than any office I'd ever been in before. As my eyes wandered around I couldn't get over how many books there were everywhere. I don't know why I was surprised to see books lining a publisher's walls, but I was. It was like entering a different world. Even though I'd started to read books as an adult, I'd never lived in a bookish environment. So many words telling so many stories and describing so many different lives, reminding me how many things there were that I knew nothing about; it was hard to imagine how the modest story of my childhood and my struggle to find a place in the world would fit in amongst them.

As we walked through the large offices the hush would occasionally be broken by background voices or the hum of a photocopier going backwards and forwards. I felt I should be walking on tiptoe for fear of disturbing people's concentration or earning their disapproval. It was then that I started to wonder just how many of the people I was passing had read what I had written. I knew this was a dream come true and I had to keep reminding myself that I'd actually written a book and that these people wanted to publish it. I was grateful, I really was, and it was a great compliment. But I now knew why I kept getting so upset; it was because I felt naked, stark bollock naked. When people glanced up from their desks as I walked past I wondered if they'd read what I'd written. Did they know all about me; my past, my present and all my future dreams? I felt I had nothing left for myself. It was as if I was parading past them with just my rucksack on my back. Was I selling my soul? Yes, I rather thought I was. I kept my head down trying not to make eye contact, and speeded up to catch up with Barbara and Lindsey, narrowly missing a filing cabinet on the way.

As we reached a large, internal, glass-walled office I noticed a man and two women inside, standing talking to each other. As we drew closer they turned and were watching us, their eyes fixed on the three of us as we went through the office door. I didn't like being the centre of attention. As I passed through the glass door I was faced with a line of people who definitely knew all about me because they had read the manuscript closely enough to want to publish it. I didn't know whether to run away or just cover my private parts. I was feeling humiliated by all the attention. I remembered Gloria and the many things she did to humiliate me so many times over the years. I tried to tell myself this was different. This was not me standing naked as a child while Gloria rained blows and abuse down on me.

As we came into the office Barbara and Lindsey moved to one side giving the three people room to come directly to me, even before greeting Barbara, hands outstretched and broad smiles. They each introduced themselves to me. There was Tom Weldon, the managing director of Penguin General Division, Louise Moore, publishing director from Michael Joseph, and Grainne Ashton, the marketing director. Barbara had already told me who I was meeting and what their functions were, but the feelings of nakedness and worries about how I was going to handle the situation were now preoccupying my mind and I was feeling extremely vulnerable.

All eyes in the room came to rest on me again as we settled down to business. The spacious office had a desk in one corner and a large oval table in the other, which was where we were all to be seated once our refreshments had been organized and the formalities attended to. I reached into my rucksack and took out the notepad and pen and placed them carefully on the table in order not to make too much noise. I then placed the rucksack between my legs. They were all smiling and being so polite, as you would expect, but still I was anxious about the way I was feeling and had visions of Gloria being in the room with me.

Their eyes remained fixed on me, even when Tom opened the meeting by saying how much they liked the book. They then went to great lengths to convince me that they would love to publish my story and explained what they would like to do and how they wouldn't put me through anything I didn't want to do. They were all being so kind and so complimentary about the book that I found it hard to take in. It seemed strange that only a few weeks before I was struggling to convince anyone of what I could do. I tried to avoid their eyes and distract myself from my feelings. I glanced around at all the books on the walls. It must have seemed as though I wasn't interested in what they were saying, but I couldn't help it. I kept seeing Gloria and some of the things she did. I started fiddling nervously with my hands in my lap, like I might have done twenty years before when I was called into the headmaster's study to be told off for some misdemeanour or when I got home and Gloria and Dennis were fighting in another room and I would huddle away in a corner trying to keep out of the way, but knowing that at any moment they would burst in and use me as a punch bag to release their frustrations.

I didn't know what else to do with myself and was becoming agitated. I was anxious to get a grip and so I tried to prove to them that everything I'd written was true and began fumbling nervously around in the rucksack, trying to get out the green folder. I was looking down, grateful to escape their eyes and all I could hear was my own voice saying, 'It's true. It's all true.' But they assured me it wasn't necessary to prove anything, that they believed me.

'We know what you've written is true,' one of the women said.

I stopped fumbling and sat back up, taking a deep breath as I tried to compose myself. I looked up and they were all still looking at me. I noticed there were tears in some of the women's eyes. I looked away again quickly, swallowing back my own emotions.

I didn't have to prove anything because they were all totally on my side but the feeling of nakedness was almost overwhelming, encouraging my emotions and visions of the past to bubble dangerously close to the surface again.

I looked up once more and realized that all the women had tears in their eyes now and my heart sank. If they all started crying I didn't think I would be able to control myself for much longer. I had no idea how to react to this sort of display of emotion. My life had always gone at such a fast pace I'd never had much of a chance to dwell on the past until I wrote the book, let alone discuss it with other people. Now, at last, I was being afforded that luxury and I wasn't sure how to handle it. Barbara smiled at me across the table and I tried to smile back. We got on to a conversation about my children and I couldn't control the rush of emotion any longer. I swung my chair round to look at the bookshelves behind me so that my face was hidden from them as I fought to compose myself. My jaw was hurting from trying to stop myself crying, but I couldn't hold the tears back any more. My eyes filled with water.

'Oh, bollocks!' I said to myself.

I could hear their words as they talked about the book

and how they worked together as a team and a family, and how they would like me to join them. I think they carried on talking about the book because they didn't know what else to say, but what else could they say? What's happened has happened. I tried to concentrate on what they were saying in order to distract myself from the emotions that their tears were stirring inside me and to allow me time to compose myself. When I felt able to turn back to face them they asked me a few questions, but I had a feeling they'd already decided what they wanted to do, even before they met me, and that they'd just wanted to check I didn't have two heads before committing themselves to publishing my book.

I was determined to answer a question they had asked about the children, but while answering I think my voice must have cracked and they all began wiping their eyes again and passing around the tissues. I felt desperate to get out of the building and into the fresh air, to be on my own with no one looking at me or knowing anything about me or feeling sorry for me. The panic was growing inside me and I wanted to gather my thoughts. Did I really want to publish this book if it was going to make me feel like this?

'Kevin is still a little unsure that he wants to do this,' Barbara warned them, as if reading my thoughts, and they immediately started reassuring me again that they would look after me and would never make me do anything I didn't feel comfortable with. They were such a nice bunch of people I could quite believe that they would do their best, but could anyone protect me from the feelings and visions that were constantly struggling to escape from inside? If I felt this emotional in a meeting of half a dozen people, how would I feel when the world was able to read the story of my life? I couldn't answer that question, nor all the others that were spinning around in my head. I stared down at my hands, picking at the skin nervously.

The effort of holding everything in was making my head hurt and suddenly, while Barbara was talking, I said, 'I want to go home now,' very abruptly.

Barbara could see that I'd had as much as I could handle and called a halt to the meeting. It felt very strange to have an agent looking after my interests; very strange but also very satisfying. We all stood up and said our goodbyes. I distracted myself again by looking at the rows and rows of books on the walls as they all made a bit more small talk before we left. But every time I looked at a book, they would give it to me. I kept protesting that they didn't have to give me things, but they insisted. As we left the building I took a huge gulp of fresh air. The gentle breeze quickly dried my eyes and cooled my face. I placed the rucksack on my back. It was now so full of books that I thought my shoulders would break, but I must admit it felt good to be given the gifts.

After saying goodbye to Barbara outside the building I felt relieved that it was all over, but my mind was already busy with questions about how I was going to be able to handle having everyone know about my life. I was excited by what was happening, but it was hard to focus on any one thought when there were so many jostling for space in my head. Would I be able to cope with interviews if this book was published? Would I be able to accept my friends and relatives knowing everything about me after having kept the secrets for so long? What if the book was a failure, how would I feel then?

It seemed like a giant leap into the unknown, partly exhilarating and partly terrifying, and if I hadn't had Jackie and Barbara on my side I don't know if I would have had the nerve to go through with it. I think without them the manuscript would have gone into a box in the attic, collecting dust, never to come out again. The emotions would have been sealed up inside me once more and I would have got on with my life doing something else.

As the meeting was held on a Friday, we now had the weekend to think about what we were doing. I imagined the people at Michael Joseph were thinking as much about whether I would be able to pull off the necessary promotional work for the book as I was. After the meeting Barbara had been as gentle as always, telling me not to worry and just to enjoy the weekend and wait to see what happened. She told me she'd never before been to an editorial meeting where everyone had tears in their eyes and she thought that must be a good sign.

Bizarre, I thought to myself.

I took the long route home to give myself time to sort out my thoughts. How was I going to deal with the feelings of nakedness? How would people react to the book? Most importantly of all, how would my brothers and sisters, and Gloria and Dennis react? I knew I had to tell my brothers and sisters what I'd written. I hadn't thought about it previously but the prospect now filled me with anxiety. What would happen if they didn't want the history of the Lewis family to be out in the open?

Jackie had picked up the children from school by the time I got back and I tried to put it all out of my mind until Monday, hoping that by then it would become obvious what should happen and how Jackie and I would deal with it.

'How did it go?' Jackie asked eagerly as soon as I came through the door.

'Really cool,' I said, 'but at one point I got a bit upset.'

She put her arms around me and hugged me tightly. My arms stayed at my side because I was still having visions of Gloria. We then got on with playing with the kids and planning what to do for the weekend. But all that was about to change.

4

The Offer

We were in the kitchen a couple of hours later, giving the kids their tea, when the phone rang. It must have been just after six o'clock, a time when you might have imagined everyone was leaving their offices for the weekend.

'Hi, Kevin, it's Barbara.' By now I instantly recognized Barbara's familiar soft voice. 'I have some fantastic news.' Even her reserved manner couldn't disguise her excitement.

'Oh, yes?' I replied, a little hesitantly.

'Michael Joseph have quadrupled their offer if we agree not to talk to any other publishers.'

'Oh,' I said, not able to take in what she was saying. 'OK.'

Her voice rose just a little, as if she realized she was going to have to explain herself more clearly. 'Kevin,' she repeated, 'this is fantastic news.'

'Cool,' I said.

She was obviously unsure how to take my lack of excitement at such an extraordinary turn of events, and was a little disappointed that I wasn't jumping around with joy. 'Well,' she said, 'think about it over the weekend and let me know what you decide on Monday.'

I put the phone down and calmly told Jackie what I'd just heard. Jackie understood the importance of the call immediately and let out an hysterical shriek of delight. She didn't need any time to let the news sink in. As she jumped about and hugged me I could see that something amazing had happened, but I still couldn't quite believe it. I was shocked and my arms were still down at my sides as I tried to work out what was going on in my head. I was beginning to smile and I could feel goosebumps travelling up my arms and down my back.

I phoned Barbara back a few minutes later, not quite sure what to say.

'Are you sure?' I asked calmly.

'Definitely,' she replied.

'That's pretty cool, isn't it?'

'Yes, Kevin,' she said, obviously relieved that the penny was finally dropping, 'it's very cool indeed. It's absolutely brilliant.'

'OK, thank you,' I said, and hung up once more.

A few minutes later I rang again. As the news was filtering a little further into my brain I was becoming more and more excited.

'This is bloody brilliant!' I said, a huge smile on my face and tingles running all over my body.

'Yes, Kevin,' she laughed, 'it is brilliant.'

Now, the anxieties and doubts I'd been experiencing, and all thoughts of how I was going to deal with what I had written were suddenly driven out of my head, replaced by a lovely new feeling of lightness, something I had never experienced before. It was as if a huge weight had been lifted from my shoulders and a feeling of security had settled in its place. Maybe, I thought, every-thing was going to be all right after all. As I thought about it more, and once the reality of what had happened had finally sunk in, my grin stretched from one end of the room to the other. Not only was my story being believed, and not only were people showing an interest in what had happened to my life before meeting Jackie, but now we had no more money worries, at least for a while. I will never forget that feeling. It was nothing short of spectacular. No more getting up each morning in order to fight just to survive, not for the foreseeable future anyway. We intended to enjoy every moment of this new-found feeling of financial security. As a family we could now plan what we wanted to do in the future to help ensure our happiness and security. I'd always wanted to be given a chance in life, now I had it and I was going to grab it with both hands.

That evening Jackie, the children and I were dancing round the kitchen we were so happy. I lifted the children into my arms as we danced to Elton John's 'Are you ready for love?' which is my daughter's and my favourite song. The kids had known that I was writing a book, although I'd told them they couldn't read it until they were at least twelve. I didn't want them to be exposed to the sort of life their dad had led until they were mature enough to handle it. Ideally, I would prefer them not to read it until considerably later, but I doubt if they will wait that long.

We spent the rest of the evening listening to Elton John and Barry White tracks blaring from the kitchen while playing around the house, chasing each other through the rooms, until we eventually wore ourselves out. That evening I lay in bed with a huge, relaxed smile on my face. Life, I decided, was bloody brilliant.

I've never been any good at lying-in, especially lately with my past making my nights so restless, but now I got up early because I didn't want to waste any of my fantastic new life. Over breakfast the next day we decided we would each buy ourselves a treat to celebrate the good news and headed off to Bluewater shopping centre. The kids both chose a toy and Jackie, much to the relief of the rest of us, said that she'd come back on her own another day to buy herself some clothes. She wanted to take her time and knew that the kids and I would be getting impatient within a few minutes.

Having sorted out the children it was my turn to decide what I was going to buy for myself and I knew straight away what I wanted. I'd always fancied an electric toothbrush. It's one of those frivolous items I could have bought many times over the years, but never got around to doing. So I decided now would be a good time to indulge myself. I went into the shop and picked up the biggest box with an all-singing, all-dancing electric toothbrush – flosser, accessories, you name it, it had it. The fact that every time I brushed my teeth with it my nose tickled and I would be continuously scratching was of course beside the point.

After we'd finished shopping we headed for the cinema, splashing out on posh seats in the sofa section and taking in giant buckets of popcorn and packets of sweets. After the film we went out to dinner and later that evening we headed home. As soon as the kids got into the car they fell into an exhausted sleep with their hats still on their heads. We drove silently home that evening, Jackie and I smiling all the way, with her hand resting reassuringly on my leg. That night I enjoyed the deepest sleep I can ever remember. Life, I decided as I drifted off, was very good indeed.

5
The Big Wait

Because the manuscript was in a finished state when it was sent to the publishers, there was very little for me to do once they'd accepted it. They wanted to make hardly any changes at all, which I was very pleased about. It would have been awful to have had to justify every scene, or to have to go back and re-write chunks of it. It made me think that perhaps I would be able to put it all behind me. But now that the project that had been filling my thoughts and my time for several months had temporarily disappeared from my life, it had left a disconcerting vacuum in its place.

The editorial staff at Michael Joseph had taken the book over and were doing whatever they had to do to prepare it for the market in seven or eight months' time. They were designing covers and briefing sales people, arranging advertising and dealing with printers – all the things that they were expert in and I knew nothing about. So there I was, sitting at home thinking of those people silently going about their business, working on my life in order to make it as pleasing as possible to the general public. It was a good feeling, a confident feeling. I would sit at home and think of all these people working on what would be called *The Kid* and a pleasant smile would spread across my face.

Occasionally I would receive a phone call or an invitation for lunch, or I would be sent something to look at, but mostly they got on with their jobs and I was left to wait until publication, which was scheduled for the following June.

The best thing about it all was that I now had the freedom to plan what I wanted to do with my future. The first thing I noticed was that, now I had the time to sit back and think properly about my choices, I began changing my ideas about what I wanted to achieve. Things I'd thought about doing, like trading in the futures markets, or working in telecommunications, believing they would get me as far away from my past as possible, no longer seemed so appealing. Now, for the first time in my life, I was actually able to choose what direction to go in, and with my past still so vivid in my memory it wasn't long before I was thinking differently about my future. I had enjoyed certain aspects of writing the book and the creativity involved in coming up with new inventions and I wanted to take both skills to the next stage.

I remembered how, as a child, I used to go to my room to try to escape the rows and the beatings, usually in vain, and would spend hours locked away, sometimes too frightened to come out. Or there would be the times when my body would feel simply too painful to move and I would stay out of the way just to give myself time to recover from whatever had happened earlier. There I would be in a dishevelled state, my clothes worn and smelling, passing the time by drawing pictures on the cold, damp, grimy walls. I used anything that would leave a mark: a nail, a piece of chalk I found on the streets or in the woods or a pencil or felt tip I'd stolen from school. Anything that would make a mark without making a sound that would tell anyone else in the house what I was up to, scribble after scribble. I would draw a life far away from where I was, a life I would dream of after watching television programmes about far-away places. The pictures would depict stories of a fantasy life that would allow my mind to escape from the stifling reality around me. Even if my body was hurting from some punishment or other, my mind was still free to wander. Because the house was in such a terrible state, with dirt and excrement and half-torn wallpaper on the walls, and because the things I drew were recognizable only to me, no one noticed or cared what I was doing. Our house was always chaotic. On the occasions that Gloria did catch me she would immediately start mocking me, screaming abuse an inch away from my face. I would try to ignore her, but this would only infuriate her further and she would then punch and kick me, knocking me on to the floor while she carried on regardless. Once she was exhausted and satisfied she would break up or throw away whatever I had been drawing with and I would have to find something new. Sometimes late at night with the small train and music I had smuggled in and hidden inside the mattress, I would listen and play on my own and continue my dreams on the wall. During the days I could see my ideas clearly amidst the mess, and at night, despite having no light, I could still picture them clearly in my head with no more illumination than the moonlight coming into the room through the uncurtained windows. Inside my mind I could always see those scribbles of a life far, far away which helped to make those walls slightly more pleasant to look at. Thinking back now I realized that what I'd been doing all those years was trying to create my own stories like the ones I saw on television.

The television screen had been my only means of escape from the reality of life with Gloria and Dennis. The programmes were often American, and the plots full of straightforward heroes and villains, people winning wars single-handed, beating the bad guys to a pulp. As I thought about those daydreams I realized that that was what I really wanted to do; I wanted to put my ideas and stories on to screens, like I had in my mind so many times as a child, lying on my bed, trying to lose myself inside my own daydreams, escaping from the violence and torture all around. Now I had the choice I naturally knew what it was I wanted to do. It was clearer than anything I had ever seen; I wanted to write and dream up stories as I did as a child. Things that had once helped me escape into a world of peace and tranquillity, today would help me escape from the visions of my past that were still haunting me. Then I wanted to put them on the big screen, just as I saw them in my head. I wanted to direct films. Knowing that was what I wanted to do was one thing, but I also had to be realistic. Could I actually do it? I wanted to convert my scribbles on the bedroom wall into film scripts. I wanted to make use of my past and turn it into something positive. The question was, how was I going to go about making that happen? It's easy enough to say that you want to be a scriptwriter or a film director; it's not so easy to make it a reality.

I also knew that I wanted to write more books and continue sketching ideas for inventions, something I had always done when ideas came to me. That would be a great life, I thought to myself. These, I knew, were long-term plans, but I had to start somewhere and I couldn't see any reason why I shouldn't start straight away. So I wrote them down in big letters in my black book – *write, direct, invent* – and underlined each one.

For the first few weeks after the deal with Michael Joseph I spun into a whirlwind of activity, my head suddenly cleared by the rush of excitement of knowing what I wanted to achieve. After dropping the kids off at school I would go to a local café for coffee and eggs. I would sit at a corner table out of the way of the other customers, jotting my ideas down in my big black book – ideas for more books and films, and designs for wild inventions. Sometimes Jackie would join me, sitting peacefully beside me as I doodled away. I might then go for a drive, listening to whatever took my fancy, clearing my head from all the ideas whirling around inside it. On returning home I would work more, sometimes taking a break in the afternoon to watch a film which I now looked at differently, studying each scene carefully, believing that one day I would write and direct those big movies myself. I would go back to work until the children came home from school, than I'd be eager to close the book and spend time with them.

I was constantly trying to force thoughts of Gloria and

my past from my mind and sometimes I could manage it for quite long stretches of time, which was a big step forward. I'd embarked on writing the book in the hope that I would clear out some of the emotional baggage that had been cluttering up my subconscious for so long, but initially I'd actually found the opposite happening. I appeared to have started a chain reaction. Every door I opened in my memory seemed to lead to several more forgotten ones. In the past I wouldn't have been able to cope with some of the emotions these memories evoked, and they were still hard to cope with, but now I hoped I wouldn't have to think about any of it again for months, not until the book was published and I had to fulfil my end of the bargain by talking to journalists and whatever else the publicity people at Michael Joseph might ask of me. For a while I could work without the baggage of the past affecting me. It was like being suspended in a strange limbo. Everything in my life had always seemed so urgent up till then, and now nothing was urgent any more. We didn't even have any money problems thanks to Michael Joseph's generous advance. It was a wonder-ful, heady feeling and every idea I came up with seemed to me to be dazzlingly brilliant.

Sometimes, in the midst of this frenzied creative activ-ity, I would be troubled with self-doubts; was I aiming too high and expecting too much of myself with all these dreams of becoming a novelist, film director and inven-tor? Could I succeed at any one of these demanding vocations, let alone all three? Was I in danger of spending the rest of my life just dreaming and hoping and never bringing anything else to fruition? The determination to prove that I was a doer and not a dreamer spurred me on to even more furious bursts of energy, sometimes working late into the night. It would be at this time that I would think most of that room where I used to be scribbling on the walls and Gloria would be there. Now, however, it was as if we were separated by thick glass so that she could see what I was doing but I couldn't hear her. She would be smashing against the glass screaming and shouting to break it down and get to me, but she couldn't. I would slowly turn towards her and she would stop and I would stare straight at her, my eyes looking at her defiantly and then turn back slowly and carry on while she erupted into another attack trying to break the glass down.

At the end of the fourth week I gave Barbara a list of things I wanted to write about and told her all about my future plans. It was then that reality bit me hard on the backside.

'Kevin,' she said, her quiet but direct tone of voice halting me in mid flow as I pitched yet another stream of ideas, 'you've got to slow down. We must at least wait and see how the first book is received before you can start selling other ideas on the strength of it. Relax and enjoy life for a bit.'

I put the phone down feeling disheartened and frustrated with myself. I realized she was right. I did have to slow down. How stupid I had been, I thought to myself. I no longer had to be paddling at full speed all the time just to stay afloat, as I'd had to do when trying to establish myself in business, and when simply trying to survive before that. Rather than grabbing every idea that came into my head and running headlong towards the goal with it, I should take some time to reflect and think things through before acting, build solid foundation blocks and take things one step at a time instead of rushing on just to get away from something in the past. Time suddenly seemed to grind to an almost unbearably slow pace; a pace that I had never been used to. The sudden freedom meant I needed even more self-control than when I was struggling.

The need to fight had gone and whereas a few weeks before that had seemed like a relief, and I had revelled in the freedom, now that Barbara had slowed me down I missed the adrenalin of constantly moving forward. I needed a channel for my get-up-and-go, and I missed the daily challenge of struggling to achieve a nice future and of getting as far away from my past as possible. I started to look back through my black book with frustration, scribbling angrily over the writing and tearing pages out. Worst of all I had visions of Gloria and Dennis laughing over my shoulder.

After my conversation with Barbara my days still started with taking the children to school; seeing them run in happily invariably brought a smile to my face. Then I would sit in the coffee shop with my black book, but it no longer mattered what I had achieved by the end of the day because none of it was going anywhere, not for a while anyhow. Success felt so close I could touch it, but I just had to wait for things to take their natural course. I truly knew what direction I wanted to take. I knew that it would take time if I was going to do things correctly, but I was still impatient. It was a complete lifestyle change, and although the result was something I had always wanted, I was finding it hard to adapt to. Then there was another feeling that I hadn't experienced before: I began to feel that I didn't deserve the advance; I hadn't worked hard enough for it; I hadn't proved I could do anything – I had just taken it and that made me feel useless. The heady feeling of freedom was slowly evolving into one of frustration and boredom. Changing speeds from a hundred miles an hour to virtual standstill was very hard to get used to and the pace was beginning to drive me insane.

I also began to feel that I had become an outsider in my own life story. Whenever someone from Michael Joseph called with a question or a request for information I jumped at the chance just to get involved again, but it never lasted for long. The call would end and I would be back on the outside of the process once more.

The days passed into weeks and the boredom and frustration grew deeper and deeper as I sat at home feeling useless. It annoyed me every time I would waste a day because it was something that went completely against everything I believed in.

As I slumped in front of the television watching DVDs I would be constantly snacking on packets of chocolate biscuits, crisps, sweets or any other stodgy food that would feel sweet and comforting as my brain went numb and I lay lifeless on the sofa, only ever moving to reach for something else to eat or for the remote control. Eventually I would feel so bloated, guilty and annoyed with myself that I would drink a pint of water straight down, wait for it to hit my stomach and then go upstairs and purge myself in the bathroom. I would then sit on the cold bathroom floor, filled with even more guilt and annoyance for what I had just done, telling myself to get a grip, that I was better than this. It was a pattern of behaviour from my past that I had thought I would never be repeating, but I didn't seem to be able to stop myself. I couldn't see any way out of the pattern I was falling into.

Ever since writing about my life I began to drink more and it wasn't long before I was consuming a bottle of red wine a night. It helped take away the visions of the past that I was so desperate to leave behind. But now I began to drink earlier in the day too. I would open up a bottle of wine just as the children came home from school, as if in reaching the end of another day I needed to reward myself for my fruitless hours, finishing it during dinner. Once the kids were safely in bed, having had their bedtime stories, I'd then open another bottle and settle back down on the sofa in front of the television, sipping, pouring and staring stupidly at the screen until I fell asleep.

I enjoyed my wine, and began to relish going out in the day to choose what I was going to drink, picking bottles that to me were tasteful and enjoyable, taking my time over making my selection. My behaviour wasn't affecting the children in any way, because if I drank too early in the day I would take vitamin C and guzzle down a pint of water. But Jackie soon noticed that I was watching a lot of television and not achieving much else with my days. I'd also started to let my appearance go, only bothering to shave once a week and wearing my scruffiest old clothes all the time because I didn't feel there was anything to dress up for. Some days I looked twenty years older than my age. Jackie's comments on my appearance and behaviour were becoming more and more frequent, but whenever she suggested I might be drinking too much I would dismiss her fears out of hand. I tried to cut down the amount I drank but when that happened vivid scenes of me aged five or six would return, and I'd watch myself as the beatings rained down on me and I tried in vain to protect myself. I never seemed able to clear them from my head. My brain was dead, my stomach bloated and I was spiralling into a cycle of self-pity and guilt, which made me drink and eat more and more. I wanted to get back up and fight, but there was nothing and no one to pick a fight with.

The fact that I was drinking so much and convincing myself that I was not getting drunk made it even worse, because what was to stop me going on to open more bottles? If I got to finish two in a day, which I occasionally did, without any ill effects, then what would be enough? Where would it end? My affection for Jackie and the kids never changed and we still laughed and joked together as we always had, but underneath the surface I felt completely useless as I watched her getting on with the job of being a wife and a mother. I knew I was getting under her feet because she would just have tidied the lounge and a few minutes later there I would be, bottle open and food on the coffee table. All week I looked forward to the weekends, when the cycle would be broken, the kids would be at home so we would be doing things together all day and my drinking and eating would go back to normal.

It wasn't long before I started opening the first wine bottle at lunchtime, instead of waiting for the end of school, and spending the afternoon in front of the television as well as the evening, one movie after another after another sliding past my brain, hardly touching the sides. My eyes and head would hurt as I attempted to supress the constant battling with the visions by the glare of the television.

I have never been a great sleeper, but this new lifestyle made things even worse. After dozing all afternoon on the couch I found I was waking up at midnight, thirsty from my daytime bingeing and feeling angry with myself for wasting another precious day, but not knowing what I could do the next day to avoid it happening again. I felt useless and imagined that I was turning into Dennis, my father. There he would be, standing with his arms out on the kitchen work surface, cigarette in one hand, glass filled with gin in the other, spending the evening steadily drinking and getting more and more angry at anyone or anything. I never got angry when I drank and in the back of my mind that made me believe I was different from him.

Then one afternoon, having drunk a whole bottle of wine within an hour, I pictured Dennis coming home from work and standing alone in the kitchen with a bottle of gin and his Elvis Presley tapes playing in the background, trying to escape Gloria's shrieking and the other stresses of his life and the chaos that reigned in the house, but this time as he turned his stocky body round to face me I saw my head was on the body of my father. I sat bolt upright spilling my drink over my clothes. My throat was sore and my teeth felt like they were covered in a layer of grit from my usual purge of lunchtime stodge and wine. My eyes were forced wide open and a tear slid down my face as a chill ran down my spine. I went straight upstairs and had a sobering shower. I had less cause to be drinking than him, I told myself, because I had a beautiful, supportive wife, not someone like Gloria shouting and screaming at me every time I turned round. My health was good, which his wasn't, and I had worked hard to achieve the freedom I had wanted for so long. There was, in other words, no excuse for messing it all up. I had to get a grip of my life. I got dressed and went downstairs.

That picture of my face on Dennis's body made me realize that I could easily be sliding down the same slippery path and that shocked me. What had happened to all the dreams I'd been nursing for so long? I was finally in a position to make them come true and I was doing the exact opposite. I was being offered an opportunity to do things that I would be able to look back on with pride at the end of my life and I was letting them all slip away. I realized I had to straighten myself out and, as always, decided the best way to do that would be to write down what my problems were so that I could see them more clearly.

'Right,' I said, deadly sober although swaying a little from the sudden movement, and I went to fetch myself a piece of paper and a pen. I sat up straight and drew a line down the middle of the pad. On one side I wrote the heading 'what I want to do' and on the other 'what I don't want to do'. I underlined both of them in thick black ink. The babble of the television started to annoy me and I switched it off so I could concentrate. The silence felt good, and I opened the window to let in some fresh air. Things were starting to clear in my head and it wasn't hard to identify the things that were wrong; I was drinking too much, eating too many of the wrong things and watching rubbish television to fill the time and to distract myself from the tedium, all of which were making the situation far worse. In a nutshell, I was bored, and this was pushing forward visions from my past. I knew I was drinking to clear them, but that was the wrong way to go about it. What I needed was something to do – a fact which I wrote in big letters at the end of the 'what I don't want to do' list.

So, what did I want to do? This wasn't hard either once I'd focused my mind. I wanted to write and direct films and continue with my scribbles and inventions, but in order to do that I needed to feel fit and well again so I could pursue my dreams effectively.

I decided to write down what I was going to do about the immediate problem of getting myself motivated and back into shape again. I considered starting by giving up the drinking and dealing with the eating disorders, but felt that would be attacking the results of my problems rather than the causes. I needed to tackle the question of what I wanted to do with my life first. Once that was sorted out it would be easier to tackle the drinking. But I knew that I couldn't go from a sofa coma back to full speed overnight. Before that could happen my mind and body needed to be fit enough to cope with the task ahead. I drank another pint of water. I was alert and sobering up fast.

The moment I had something to focus my mind on I found I was able to contemplate the idea of filling my days more constructively and consequently cut out the drinking. I formed a plan; since one of my favourite drinks is ice-cold water, I made sure that during the day the wine glass I always used had iced water in it instead of wine. I decided that I would allow myself a couple of glasses of wine in the evening if I had achieved something during the day. If I hadn't achieved anything, then I wasn't allowed to drink. I realized that up till then I had largely been drinking because I hadn't achieved anything, which I could see was the wrong way to be going about things.

I tried to stick to three meals a day, which was hard in the afternoons when I was used to gorging myself. Instead of sweets, biscuits, chocolate pie and every other sort of junk food, I started making myself salads. I'd go to the fridge and throw together rocket, tuna, sweetcorn, cubed tomatoes and cucumber in a bowl with salad cream. I found my appetite just as easily satisfied, my stomach not as bloated and my brain not dead, so I could carry on working and thinking through the afternoons without falling into a sofa coma. If I found myself starting to fancy a drink in the afternoon I would get out of the house, going for a walk or for a drive and taking a bottle of water and my music with me, distracting myself from the idea of drink.

The most important thing was to get back into a routine and so I got up at six thirty every weekday morning and shaved every other day. My beard isn't heavy enough to have to do it every day, so there was no point in making my skin sorer than it needed to be, but I wanted to look smart and fresh again. After dropping the kids at school I only allowed myself to go for coffee every other day. Afterwards I would do some exercise so that by ten thirty the blood was pumping and I was ready for work.

I began by going for walks each morning along a route I already knew and liked, and then I started running part of the way. Each day I ran a bit more of the route, building my stamina and fitness gradually. At first, believing I would find running boring, I tried taking music with me, but I found it annoyed me. It interrupted my thoughts, which seemed to flow faster and faster as I ran, my heart racing.

Although I had joined a gym to use the treadmill, I found I preferred being outside, filling my lungs with fresh air, looking at the scenery, feeling the blood pumping through my veins and clearing my head, making my thoughts more fluid.

As my mind became more stimulated my body no longer seemed to need any wine. My mind and body were telling me they didn't want it and so I only drank water. My sleeping patterns improved, making me feel more alert during the day. I also found that I was now better able to get on top of my emotions. I was no longer getting upset about my past, and the old childhood habits – like stuffing my food in too fast and fussing about with my cutlery – were retreating back into their boxes once more. My subconscious was begging me to rebuild the barriers that had helped me through the early years of my life. The visions and feelings of my childhood started to float away and Gloria wasn't around me any more. I would sometimes think of her while running and it would just spur me on to run faster. The faster I ran the quicker I pictured her turning away and disappearing.

Now that I was getting back in control of my life I could see that I had the sort of successful family life that most people could only dream of, which gave me an even firmer springboard from which to have a successful career. I was very honest with myself and admitted that my biggest flaw was that I would always rush into things. Now I didn't have to do that any more. I decided I would take my time, plan my future correctly and not dash around as if I still had to make enough money every day to feed us and pay the rent. This time I was planning for my family as well as for myself.

Just shaving wasn't going to be enough to smarten me up; I was going to have to tackle the way I dressed too. Taking a roll of black bin sacks with me one afternoon I headed for my wardrobe, starting with a favourite old green jacket, which I knew Jackie particularly disliked.

'What are you doing?' Jackie asked, having got home with the kids from school to find me pushing clothes into bags.

'Moving on,' I told her and she walked up behind me, stroked my back, smiled at the sight of the green jacket in the bag and went back downstairs, leaving me to it.

I then made a more detailed list of what I should do next. I wanted to write scripts, but first I needed to establish that I could create the right framework for the kind of films that I enjoyed. I made a promise that I would be brutally frank with myself. If something I wrote was a load of rubbish, then I had to admit it and move on to something else. My main criteria for judging my work was, would it be a film that I would want to watch or not? If I didn't want to watch it myself, how could I expect other people to?

My black sketchbook was filling up with storylines and I was happy to be replacing the ones I had torn out in anger. Now plot after plot was growing and expanding as I worked harder and faster, the blood pounding round my head after the running. I would punctuate my efforts on the scripts with drawings and descriptions of inventions; everything from ways to power a house to DNA missiles, from bringing G3 bandwidth together to install in offices to a device that would go on the front of trains in order to scan the tracks ahead for abnormalities. I have always found that my mind is coming up with possible solutions to problems I come across in daily life or triggered by something I might read in the papers. I didn't always know what I wanted to do with the inventions, but I believed it was important to record them, so that I would remember them later. My brain was alive and buzzing once more. I was able to move on.

My mind and body were fit once more and I felt it was time for me to embark on the successful career I had always wanted. I sketched out my career plan on paper, breaking it down bit by bit so that I could see exactly what I needed to do. I would need training in how to write the scripts properly and in the skills needed to become a film director. I started to enquire at colleges, universities and film schools, asking them to send their prospectuses. A few days later I would be waiting impatiently for the post. These glossy and informative brochures looked slick and professional and I would take them with me on the school run and on to the café, poring over them as I had my coffee and eggs, trying to see how they could help me realize my dream. In every brochure, however, there was always a paragraph that would puncture my bubble. They all said they needed a certain level of education; GCSEs, A levels, degrees, or experience in the industry, none of which I had. No one wanted to attract students who had left school with no qualifications at all. I wasn't going to give up at the first hurdle, however, and so I called each of them in turn to see if there was any possibility that I could do one of their courses anyway. I knew I had the necessary ability. I love learning and I knew this was what I wanted to do more than anything. But they were having none of it. I simply couldn't get on these courses unless I had the relevant qualifications or experience. When I asked them how I was to get experience without the training their answers were always evasive. But having been rejected several times still didn't dissuade me, and the recurring image of me painstakingly scratching away on the walls as a child made my resolve stronger. 'I'll show them,' I said to myself. 'I'll bloody show them.'

While I was searching for a college that would accept me, I kept up my self-educating activities. I love movies about heroes; the sort of people who I remember seeing as a child; people who overcame evil and fought for what was right; the sort of characters and plots that I had been scribbling about on the bedroom walls all those years ago. I made a list of the films I'd liked over the years and found out who the directors were. I searched out their scripts on the Internet, printing them out continuously for two days, only going out of the house in order to buy more paper and ink. Then I began to study their work, deconstructing the scripts as closely as any undergraduate film student. I watched the films on the screen at the same time as reading the scripts, to see how the directors had translated the words from the page into moving images. I became fascinated by what was on the page, each scene broken down, every word and every camera angle: internal, external, wide angle, mid shot, close-up, extreme close-up. A whole new world was opening up to me and it made me hungry for more.

The first script I read was *Raiders of the Lost Ark*; a film that meant an enormous amount to me in my teenage years. I also pored over the scripts of the films *Titanic*, *Gladiator*, *Swordfish*, *Dog Day Afternoon*, *Black Hawk Down*, *Pulp Fiction*, *Devil's Advocate*, *Ronin* and *Austin Powers*; and on and on it went. I researched all the film-makers who were successful in the areas that interested me, directors like Ridley Scott, Steven Spielberg, George Lucas, John Frankenheimer and Quentin Tarantino.

I needed to be realistic about what I could and couldn't do. I was never going to be great at writing comedy, for instance, or romance. What I knew I wanted to do was make action thrillers, in both my novels and scripts, and the only way I would be able to prove I could write would be to just get on with it. So that was what I did, slowly building the blocks to storylines that I hoped would later be transformed into novels and film scripts. Every so often I would remember what all those people at the colleges had told me over the phone. Was I really aiming too high? Was I dreaming? But every time I thought that way it would spur me on further to prove them wrong.

After the confused feelings and visions of the previous eighteen months and the adjustment of one minute trying to do a hundred things at once and the next sitting in front of the television and just waiting for the book to come out, it seemed that I was now back in control of my life again. The way I looked at it was if *The Kid* was a hit that would be a bonus, but I was still going to be busy and successful even if it sank without a trace. Barbara had made sure I understood what a risky business publishing is and how many books never earn enough to even pay back the advances that the publishers hand out. Although everyone at Michael Joseph was being incredibly optimistic, I knew there was a chance it wouldn't work and I would never earn another penny from it. I needed to get on with my life as if I hadn't written the book at all. That way I would be able to put my past behind me.

During this period we were living in rented accommodation. This was a situation that always made me feel a little insecure and so I began to keep a lookout for a house that might be suitable for us. I knew I couldn't afford the farm I'd always dreamed of, but I still wanted us to own our own home. Jackie and I discussed it and we both decided that we wanted something that needed some attention so that we could put our own mark on it, just as we had eventually done in Coulsdon. Finding a good-sized house in need of refurbishment, though, was not easy. It never is, because everyone else is after the same thing. A property developer had once told me that the only way to be successful in residential property was to be able to move faster than everyone else when the right property came on the market. That meant going round the estate agents regularly so they got to know your face, grew to like you and to know that you were serious about buying – building a rapport so that you would be one of the first calls they would make when a new property came on to their books. I had been keeping my eye out for a good property, and as we had nothing to sell we were in a position to move very fast if the right one came up.

That advice and our persistence paid off because after a few months of chasing the agents one rang to say that he'd just been instructed on a four-bedroom, nineteen-thirties detached house in exactly the right condition. A proposed sale had just fallen through after the buyer pulled out at the last moment. It was occupied by an older woman who'd been there for forty or so years and now wanted to move to something smaller and more manageable. He told me I could be the first to see it if I went round immediately. The call was pure music to my ears. I jumped into the car and went to see it straight away. As soon as I drove past the property I knew it would be right. I went in to meet the seller, who was living there with her grandson. It was obvious that the house was now too big for her and she was anxious to move. She told me she'd been messed about by a previous buyer and, as soon as she'd showed me around, I gave her my word that I would buy it from her before Christmas for the price we agreed that day. I'd always made a point of keeping my word on deals, believing it pays to be trustworthy. In the past my word had been all I had to trade with in business since I had no track record and no qualifications. The deal went ahead from there with no hitches, so I knew the house would be waiting for us to start work on as soon as Christmas was over.

I was feeling very positive about life at every level, and my confidence grew stronger each day as my past faded further away. I decided that once the festive season was over I would tell my brothers and my sisters what I had written. I didn't want to leave it too close to publication date, in case they had any problems with it. I had no idea how they would react to having all our dirty washing aired in public, and I had even less idea how Gloria and Dennis would react. Was I doing the right thing by raking it up again after all these years? I was finding it hard to cope with it myself let alone the thought of telling the perpetrators of my childhood pain and suffering.

In the weeks before Christmas, however, things would happen which would change my perceptions of everything once again.

6

Voices from the Past

My mobile must ring a dozen times a day as I chat to Jackie, Barbara and all the other people who make up my daily life. It's a great tool – I love it – but now and then it brings unpleasant surprises.

It had already rung a couple of times that evening, but the caller had hung up as soon as I answered as if they'd lost their nerve at the last moment. I didn't take much notice, assuming they would either pluck up the courage to eventually speak, or else the call would not be important enough to worry about. When it rang again while I was putting the children to bed, I answered it with my usual breeziness and was shocked to hear Dennis's subdued tones. I recognized his shy, muffled voice immediately, even though I hadn't heard it for several years. I was completely unprepared for receiving a call from him, especially as not so long before I had been shaken by the image of myself turning into him. My first reaction was, had he heard about the book already? How could he have done, I thought, dismissing the idea.

I couldn't picture him using a phone at all, least of all for him to make a call to me. It turned out he'd got my number from one of my sisters, all of whom I kept in contact with on a fairly regular basis.

Listening to him I was suddenly transported back again to my childhood. The memories of how hard he would hit me – just as if he was fighting another man – sent a chill through my whole body. I tried to put all other thoughts out of my mind by concentrating on his words, which were almost too quiet and subdued for me to be able to catch them. He told me that my younger brother, Robert, who I had seen only a few times since I left home, had turned up in his life. On the odd occasions that I had spoken to my other brother Wayne, or my sisters, they'd told me that Robert would sometimes just arrive back in their lives out of the blue, regaling them with tales of all his recent adventures. They had described to me how he often seemed to be wrapped up in a world of his own, unbothered by anyone or anything beyond his own immediate needs, and how he fantasized about things. He'd always been inclined to embroider the truth somewhat in the telling of tales, even as a child, which I guess was his way of escaping from the harsh realities of his life, both past and present. Quite often, the others complained, he seemed only to have made contact with them in order to ask for money for food or a bed for the night.

Although none of them had any money to spare, they would try to help him in any way they could. He would always promise to repay them but never managed to do it, living as he did from hand to mouth. Being in such a vulnerable position apparently didn't appear to bother him. Robert's philosophy always seemed to be that if you ignored a problem for long enough it would eventually go away. Sometimes, of course, that approach works, but most of the time it merely allows the problem to grow, or turns it into someone else's. But from what I could make of it all, he seemed pretty harmless, and more like a lost child than anything else. I tried to listen carefully to what Dennis was saying about him and put my reservations aside.

Gloria had always hated Robert with much the same ferocity that she had hated me and, once I was out of the way, having finally been removed by social services from the house, he had been left to face the brunt of her anger and violence. That gave us some sort of bond and I must admit to having a soft spot for Robert even though we hadn't seen each other for so long. After I was taken into care I used to visit home at weekends and noticed that he had disappeared from the house. I paid little attention to his absence at the time, being more concerned about my own problems and knowing that it was those who were left behind at the house who had the most to worry about.

I knew from my sisters that as a young man he'd been drifting aimlessly through life, working for funfairs, jumping from job to job, unable to settle anywhere for long and sometimes living on the streets, but they were unsure how much of what he told them was fact and how much was fantasy – or at least exaggerated fact.

Since all the information about Robert had come to me secondhand I didn't want to form any judgements, but it seemed likely that he was dealing with the demons of our childhood in a very different way from me. Having not seen him for so many years I was keen to hear some firsthand news of my baby brother, particularly as his reappearance in my life coincided with me thinking about our past so much.

Dennis told me that Robert had recently been living out on the streets and in hostels and had been in and out of hospital over the previous few weeks due to an old injury on his arm. His explanations were a bit slurred and confused. It was obvious he had been drinking and I couldn't quite work out what had happened, but it seemed that he was telling me the doctors had had to take a plate from a previous injury out of Robert's arm but, because he was living rough on the London streets, the resulting wound kept going septic and wouldn't heal.

'He's been asking if you could help him,' Dennis told me. 'Christmas is coming and he hasn't got any money, but he can't sign on because he's in hospital . . .'

Robert and I had been through a lot together when we were little and I'd always felt it was my job to protect him, particularly on the occasion that he fell into the clutches of a paedophile when he was too young to know what to do about it, so there was no way I would turn my back on a direct plea for help from him now. I told Dennis I would go to the hospital the following day to see him, feeling very unsure what I would find when I got there. We said our goodbyes and I must admit my hands and legs were shaking as I put the phone down. I remembered so much of what he did to me as a child that it seemed strange to be talking to him about helping my brother, as if everything was normal between us. That night I thought a lot about how this quiet, shy man would burst into black rages, his anger fuelled by drink and aggravated by the uncontrollable chaos which filled the house.

The following day, as I travelled into London to see Robert, I felt a lot of conflicting emotions. Pictures of him as a child kept coming into my mind. The last time I had seen him was over five years ago, when he was in his early twenties. I was looking forward to seeing him again, although at the same time I bore in mind the warnings from my other brother and sisters. I felt excited but wary about how he might have changed in the intervening years.

From the moment he left home Robert had been living from one moment to the next, never thinking beyond the next few minutes, never able to make a plan or see a way to improve his lot in life. If he'd had a meal or a drink or a few pounds in his pocket then that was all he needed until that little bit of money ran out or his hunger or thirst returned. He had no idea how to support himself or move past the damage that had been inflicted on him at the beginning of his life. I was hoping that now we were back in contact I would be able to help him change this dangerous pattern of behaviour; help him make plans and look to the future. I found so much comfort in looking forward rather than backwards and I wanted him to be able to do the same. I believed that if he could do that then he would be able to see the possibility of a more comfortable and satisfying life, just as I had done as a young man, and that that would drive him forward to make more of an effort to get some stability in his life.

I felt increasingly nervous once I arrived in the alien, sterile environment of the hospital, trying to find my way around the endless corridors with their confusing signs. When I finally reached the door of his room I opened it slowly, unsure what I would discover on the other side. The first thing I saw was this fragile young man lying in the hospital bed. His vulnerability shocked me, knocking the wind out of my chest as I walked into the room. I tried to act casually, as if my visit was the most natural thing in the world. I took a deep breath and smiled, unable to think what to say. Even though he was twenty-seven years old he looked like a little lost boy, as if all strength and life had been drained from him and he had no fight left.

When he saw me a weak smile almost lit up his face and I felt a genuine glow of pleasure at the sight of someone who had come from the same place as me, who understood what it felt like to live as we had lived, who shared so many experiences and feelings, memories and fears. I loved him, as I did my other brother and sisters, and when I looked at him lying in the bed, attached to a drip, too exhausted to cope any more, I could see myself as I might have been if things had turned out differently. My emotions were still dangerously raw from revisiting all my childhood experiences and the sight of this sick, damaged, exhausted boy brought them painfully back to the surface. During that first hospital visit the conversation was slow and sometimes awkward. There were long silences between us as we both stared at the television, desperately trying to think of things to say to each other. Although it was uncomfortable, we were both happy to be in each other's company and that was enough for now.

I visited him regularly in the coming days and he

seemed to be growing stronger and happier with each visit, a bit of colour creeping back into his cheeks as he chatted up the nurses. We started talking about his recent adventures, his girlfriend, his time working on the funfairs and about a bit of trouble he'd had with the law. It seemed he'd never stayed anywhere for long, and never managed to organize himself to get a permanent place to live, even when the alternative would be a night spent in a cold shop doorway.

'Why don't you stay with Dennis?' I asked.

'I do sometimes,' he said, 'but it isn't easy.'

He told me how things between them would be fine during the early parts of the day, but the more Dennis drank the angrier and more aggressive he became, kicking and swearing at Robert and venting all of his pent-up emotions and frustrations, just like when we were children and he had to live with Gloria.

'Why don't you defend yourself against him?' I wanted to know. 'You're a man now; you're stronger than him. You don't have to take that sort of thing any more.'

'He might chuck me out of the flat and I wouldn't have anywhere else to go,' he admitted. I could see how hard he found it to stick up for himself in any situation.

I wasn't surprised to hear how Dennis had behaved towards him because I'd heard from the others that he still drank. We all knew how emotional and angry he could become when drunk, although I had hoped time might have mellowed him. At the back of my mind, however, the warnings the others had given me about Robert's tendency to exaggerate kept nagging away. As I listened to him talking about Dennis I wanted to believe

Robert was overstating the facts and that Dennis was not still the miserable, vicious drunk he had been during our childhood, but I had no way of judging. Later that day, once I had returned home, I spoke to one of my sisters on the phone, asking if Robert's stories were likely to be true.

'It may be that Dennis did get angry with him on a couple of occasions,' she replied, 'but only because Robert kept using the flat as if it was his, never making any effort to get a place of his own. Dennis would get fed up with it.'

It seemed there might be two sides to these stories. Robert, I realized, was no longer a helpless child and couldn't automatically expect his father's protection against the world. On top of that, Dennis was the wrong sort of person for anyone to look to for protection. On the other hand, caring for Robert could have given Dennis some opportunity to make up for the terrible childhood he had given us all.

Arriving at the hospital one afternoon for my regular visit, I could see Robert had been badly shaken by something.

'Gloria's been in,' he said.

'Is she still here?' I wanted to know, immediately feeling myself starting to shake at the possibility of bumping into her. I thought about the room in my visions with the glass panel separating us and imagined her smashing it down to get to me.

'No, she came earlier.'

'What did she want?'

'Money. She told me she was in here visiting a friend, so she thought she'd see if I had any money. I could hear her coming from miles away. She was shouting and yelling and swearing down the corridors. I tried to get into the bathroom to hide, but I couldn't make it in time because of this.' He gestured at the drip that he was still having to waddle around with wherever he went. We both laughed at the image of Robert in his hospital nightie, stumbling around as he tried to hide from the terrible roar of his approaching mother.

'You didn't give her anything, did you?' I asked sternly.

'No,' he shook his head vehemently.

Even though we were laughing I could see that he was hurt to think his own mother would only come to see him in hospital in order to cadge money off him. Everyone would like to think that whatever else, at least they're loved by their mothers. It was a luxury he would never experience. That lack of love didn't bother me any more. I never treated her like a mother anyway. I had Jackie and the kids to love me and to love in return. Robert, I realized, was still searching for someone to fill that void and, deep down, I could sense that he still missed a mother figure.

Jackie had told me in the past, after speaking to Gloria on the odd occasion, that she had always had something bad to say about Robert. She was still putting him down. Even after all these years she couldn't leave him alone. Knowing how the filth was always pouring out of her mouth, I hadn't attached much importance to it, but her continuing hatred and contempt for her youngest son after so many years seemed all the more poignant now that I was with him and could see how vulnerable he was. Although Jackie had always been polite to Gloria, until she read the book and found out the truth, she had also tried to steer her away from talking Robert down. She didn't like to hear any mother bad-mouthing her own children, but Gloria was unperturbed. Unkindness came too easily to her, even now when she apparently needed and wanted contact with her children and grandchildren more than ever.

'I spoke to Dennis on the phone and he says he'll put you up when you come out,' I told him. 'But behave yourself.'

'What do you mean?' he wanted to know.

'Just behave yourself,' I said again, and I think he understood what I meant, even if he didn't want to admit it. I then told him that as soon as he got out of hospital we'd organize some more permanent accommodation for him. I also suggested that while he was in hospital he should write a plan of what he wanted to do with himself, both in the short term when he was discharged, as well as in the medium term over the next year or two, and finally in the long term.

'Just be free to write whatever you want,' I told him, jotting the words 'short, medium and long term' on a piece of paper and leaving it on his cabinet.

I was already hatching a plan myself that might take care of his short-term problems. As the house I was buying needed some improvements and modernization, the work would require another pair of hands, and I thought Robert would be the ideal person to help me. It would also give him somewhere to live while he sorted out what he wanted to do next. It seemed the perfect fit.

'I'm going to be buying a house which will need doing up,' I told him. 'Fancy coming to help after Christmas? It's a nice house, just a bit tired, perfectly liveable in though. You could stay there and help me work on it if you like.'

'Yeah,' he said, his eyes brightening. He seemed genuinely excited at the prospect of us doing something as brothers, and I began to think that perhaps together we could find a way to extricate him from the poverty trap that he seemed unable to get out of on his own.

During the time that I was visiting the hospital, Dennis started ringing me regularly on the pretext of discussing Robert's situation. I could tell that he wanted to talk to me about more personal things, but I couldn't bring myself to go beyond the cold, practical details of arrangements and plans. I remained firm and to the point, unable to open myself up to anything sensitive or emotional with him. With no encouragement from me he was too shy to say what he was thinking. As long as we were discussing Robert's welfare there was a reason for us to be speaking. Without that reason I would have been unable to do it. I could never simply have phoned him to find out how he was or chat about the past. It would have been unthinkable, raising far too many of the uncomfortable memories that I had been trying to lock back up.

Did he feel bad about the past or did he even think he did anything wrong? I wasn't sure and, to be honest, I didn't want to find out.

I knew from Robert that Dennis seldom went out any

more, not even to the pub. He spent his days alone in his flat, drinking, becoming progressively more confused, slurred and angry as the hours slipped by. Eventually he would slip into unconsciousness, waking sober the next morning and starting the whole destructive cycle all over again. If we spoke early in the day his voice was almost normal, but if he phoned me later his tongue would be clumsy from the alcohol. I felt irritated by this reminder of why, as a young man, he had so often been unable to put right what went wrong in our family life. In our conversations on the phone the drink would make him upset and very emotional, and he would often cry, wallowing so deeply in self-pity it would be hard to follow the rambling course of his speech. I would end the calls as quickly as possible, not knowing how to respond to these slurred emotional outpourings. It reminded me of how emotional he would get in the kitchen. We were so used to it as kids that we didn't take any notice and, annoyed that we wouldn't feel sorry for him, he would lash out.

It was impossible for me to deal with his demons when I was still trying to cope with the ones that had been stirred up inside my own head. The last thing I wanted was to have to listen to a drunken Dennis crying down the phone to me. It was too soon to be dealing with such emotive, personal issues when we had only just started communicating again. During our conversations I made a point of hardly mentioning Jackie and the children, fearful of driving him into an even more emotional state. Listening to his moaning made me angry, which in turn made me feel guilty for being unsympathetic. But it was the only way I could handle this onslaught of emotion from a man who had often beaten me so badly that I would be in pain for days. If Jackie or the children became emotional about things I knew how to handle it, hopefully providing them with the love and support they needed. But this was a grown man who had never given a thought in the past to how his actions were damaging the lives of the six children who were forced to live with him in that little tin house.

Thinking back now, it's possible he had been giving some thought to the damage he had done, and that realization was part of the reason why he was becoming so upset now. Was this what made him drink so much? I don't know. He'd been a heavy drinker ever since I could remember. Whatever the reason, I didn't feel ready to find out; I just wanted to distance myself from him again. His barrage of emotions pushed me away. After his calls I always had trouble sleeping as my mind chewed over every word he had said, wondering if I was doing the right thing in writing about him. But then the memories would come back and I would remember when I was at home and he would burst in to the room after he and Gloria had had a fight. Spurred on by Gloria, who would have told him something bad about me out of pure hatred, he would head straight for me. The blood would drain from my face before the first blow even fell, defeated by sheer fear. Knowing what was coming I would curl up in a ball on the cold, dirty floor to try to protect myself, but he would straighten me out as easily as unfolding a piece of paper and then lay into me with punches, kicks, and lashes with his belt buckle or anything else that came to hand. I would be screaming with pain and limp. My brothers and sisters would be all around screaming for him to stop while Gloria towered behind them, fag in mouth, smiling.

Although I only called him in the mornings when he was more likely to be sober enough to control his emotions, I couldn't always block his calls to me later in the day. There was one evening when I couldn't avoid taking his call. Knowing that he would have been drinking for several hours by then, eager to get back to reading the children their bedtime stories and resenting the intrusion into our private time together, I struggled to keep the conversation matter-of-fact. It was near the end of Robert's stay in hospital, and I was trying to explain to Dennis what would happen, when he suddenly said something I'd never heard him say before.

'I love you.'

His voice was muffled, but the words were quite pronounced.

I didn't know what to do. It took me aback, shocked me and a host of butterflies took flight in my stomach. I put the phone down, quite unable to think of anything to say in response. I finished reading to the children, my mind a million miles away from the story, and kissed them goodnight. There had been so many years that I'd longed to hear those words from him or Gloria, especially after school or during the long miserable, frightening nights, when the pain would seem overwhelming and I would be desperate for help and some sign of hope. I'd built so many barriers over the years that when the words finally did arrive I had no way of dealing with them. Once I was downstairs I stood staring at the phone, the butterflies having returned again, as I tried to work out what I should do. Should I call him back and respond to the words? Should I just leave it?

I left it. It was just too hard to deal with. So many contradictory thoughts and emotions were swirling around my head that it was safer that way. How could I respond after so many painful, desperate years, so many blows raining down on me, one after another after another, my screams and pleas for mercy making no difference to the ferocity of his attacks? How could three little words possibly wipe out all the years of memories? I'd always believed I was his favourite from little looks he had given me and the odd reassuring pat on the back when things were going badly. He seemed to show some favouritism towards me when it came to taking one of us to the pub with him. I liked those outings when it was just him. I would wait anxiously while he got ready to go and if I didn't think he was going to take me I would scream to be taken, to get away from Gloria. Although he took me more than the others, he mostly went on his own, leaving me with her. Once he was gone I would stop screaming, knowing what was going to happen next. She would immediately be shouting at me, her face within an inch of mine.

'Daddy's fucking little boy, are you? Fucking queer,' she would mock me as she got herself into such a frenzy mainly because she knew I didn't want to be with her. Then she would lay into me. I'm sure Dennis could hear the screams of pain as he walked away from the house.

Knowing I was his favourite made her hate me all the

more ferociously. It was a catch-22, because it made her work even harder in her attempts to turn him against me when he was drunk and feeling angry at the whole world. The moment he got home she would start telling him all the things I'd done wrong.

'Do you want to know what *your* fucking cunt of a son has done now?'

Even though Dennis had never had any idea how to show his affection properly or how to protect me, Gloria knew he was fond of me, so she would egg him on to attack me. Despite knowing all this, it was still a shock to hear him say something so personal. I was assailed by doubts as to whether or not I was being fair in writing the book and exposing this sad, sick old man's short-comings as a father. Was I doing the right thing? Had he been doing his best all those years? Had beating me into submission been the only way he could cope?

By showing concern for Robert, and trying to help him, it looked as if Dennis was finally attempting to make amends for all the times when he didn't help us as children, but then he was still attacking Robert when he had had too much to drink, just as he always had with all his children. During my hospital conversations with Robert I found out that Dennis had suffered three strokes, which had muffled his voice and personality even further than in his youth, but did his failing health mean he should be forgiven for everything he had done, or failed to do, in the past? I truly didn't know the answers to any of these questions and so there was nothing to stop them spinning round and round in my head, keeping me awake at night and distracting me during the day. What made it worse was that when I did talk to him a tidal wave of emotions far too big for me to handle came rushing in. Robert and Dennis, I decided, would just have to sort things out between themselves over the Christmas period. Despite all their problems, I suspect they were both grateful for one another's company over the festive season.

I still hadn't told anyone in the Lewis family about the book, but I knew that sooner or later I was going to have to come clean if I didn't want them to feel betrayed when it appeared in the shops and they had to hear about it at the same time as the rest of the world. I was nervous about introducing the subject to anyone, friend or relative.

'I've written a book,' I imagined myself saying.

'Really,' they would say politely. 'What's it about?'

'Oh, it's about my abused childhood,' I would have to reply, and the conversation would then grind to an embarrassed and embarrassing halt. But I knew I would have to tell them after Christmas.

Christmas was wonderful. As always I was even more excited than the children as we traced Father Christmas's footsteps around the house, opened presents, played games and did all the silly things you do at that time of the year. I left Dennis and Robert to look after one another. I knew it wasn't the ideal situation, but I also knew that I'd done all I could for the moment and once the holiday season was over we could concentrate on trying to get Robert settled somewhere permanently.

7

Bringing Us Closer Together

After Christmas I felt refreshed and eager to start work on the renovation of the house and was looking forward to spending time with Robert. I was hugely enjoying all the reading, writing and studying involved in learning about films and working on my own storyboards and inventions, but I felt it would be the best of all possible worlds if I could break the bouts of intense concentration up with sessions of manual labour, working on the house myself alongside Robert and other tradesmen. The rush of physical labour would get the blood pumping through me and stimulate my thoughts even further.

The house had had nothing done to it for years and needed some tender loving care to bring it back to its original condition. It was still perfectly habitable and would be a home for Robert while it was being refurbished, which would hopefully help him get on his feet and out of Dennis's way. It would also give us time to find him a home of some sort so that he could get himself off the streets and out of the night hostels once and for all. I liked the idea of finding him somewhere close to us so we could spend time together, which was something we'd never been able to do before. I was also looking forward to helping him move on, showing him that he could have a better life if he wanted one. Little did I know how hard that would actually be.

A few days after the festive season Robert had moved into the house and we set to work. The man I had put in charge of the project was a friend of mine, who I called 'Little Mark'. I'd worked with him on our other house and knew he was a really good builder and an incredibly hard worker.

We started by gutting the building completely. Within a week we'd filled five skips with rubbish, having brought the house back to its bare walls. From there we worked together putting in a new kitchen and bathrooms, plastering, electrics, staircase, everything that brought life back to this family home. For four months Mark and I worked solidly from eight in the morning to four in the afternoon. I no longer had to worry about going for runs because now I was getting more than enough exercise mixing cement, plastering and plumbing.

In the evenings, once the kids were in bed, I would spend a few hours working on the film scripts and continuing my efforts to find somewhere I would be accepted to train to become a film director. My brain was clear from all the physical activity of the day, which in turn helped me sleep better at night. It was a great feeling. During this time I realized that I actually enjoyed pressure. When it had been taken away by the success of the book deal I had missed it. Now I was able to reapply it with my own self-imposed budgets and deadlines, setting myself targets to get the house completed on time and searching for a place for me to study film making.

My relationship with Robert over this period, however, was to be turbulent to say the least.

8

Brotherly Love

During the months we were working on the house Robert would come and go. To begin with our relationship went well, the three of us laughing and joking all the time, with Robert and Mark exchanging jokes and taking the mickey out of one another's taste in radio stations. When one wasn't looking the other would change stations, which would inevitably lead to a water fight or some other act of revenge. I was looked upon as the serious one and they would try to involve me in their playful banter. I became persuaded to start laying booby traps for one or other of them, like buckets of water placed precariously on top of ajar doors, drenching the victim and ending up with me being chased around the house with whatever weapon they had in their hands at the time. I did get my come-uppance now and then, since they were never convinced by my threats of non-payment. It was a good time. We worked hard and we had fun in a way Robert and I had not been able to do when we were growing up. All three of us were bonding well and the house was steaming ahead at full speed, which was just how I liked it.

When Robert was there we both enjoyed working together and getting to know one another better. We never talked about the past at all. It seemed as though nothing had ever happened. This made me hesitant to bring up the subject of what I had written.

Within three weeks of being in the house, however, I was clearly seeing the other side of Robert's character. Whenever he had a little money in his pocket I knew he wouldn't want to work the next day. He'd always lived that way. It annoyed me to start with and I tried to make him realize that to give himself a future he had to start thinking ahead and that this was a great opportunity for him to get his life in order. But I soon realized I wasn't going to change him. I either accepted the way he was or I didn't. There was no other choice. The idea of listing his goals, for instance, was too alien for him to grasp. When I asked him if he had done it he just responded with a sullen silence.

There were bound to be days when our different approaches to life would cause us to fall out. Sometimes, for instance, Robert would pretend he could do something that he couldn't, and would end up making a complete mess of a job which we would then have to spend days putting right. He didn't mean any harm by it, but what was getting to me was that my brother just didn't want to look ahead. If he did, it would be to dream up some huge, grand plan of how he was going to travel around Australia, which was great, but if I then asked him how he was going to pay for it and whether he planned to get a permanent job and save for his dream, he would just go quiet and retreat inside himself. By asking practical questions I had pricked his bubble. It reminded me of times in my room as a child when the dreams and stories that I been creating inside my own bubble would be burst with a loud bang whenever Gloria or Dennis came into the room and attacked me. Afterwards I would lie there in pain, knowing they could never actually stop the dreams flowing inside my head. With Robert it was like dealing with a kid who has no idea about the realities of life, but still wants to believe that his dreams will come true, which is what has always helped me. I saw that the main difference between us was that, although I also had my dreams of writing and becoming a film director, which might seem far-fetched to some people, I was breaking them down bit by bit and then building the blocks to my goals. Robert didn't want to look at the practicalities of how to achieve his dreams.

On one occasion when he completely messed up a room, I really lost my temper, yelling at him that he should stand up straight and face the world. I told him to accept responsibility for his actions and sort his life out. All my tirade did though was make him turn even deeper inwards and walk off the site. I immediately felt bad for attacking him and becoming annoyed because he wouldn't change rather than accepting him and being supportive and encouraging. I'd always known we were different, but I hadn't realized quite how wide the gulf between us was until that point. I love all my brothers and sisters and I knew Robert was dealing with his past in the best way he could. I desperately wanted to help him get on and to see that there is a better life if you work hard at it, but I couldn't do it on my own. He needed to want that better life himself; he needed to help himself before anyone else could do anything. I knew that he wanted to achieve something in life, as we all do, but he wanted to do it in his own way, not mine. We always made up shortly after our squabbles and I soon realized that he couldn't do things any differently, any more than I could. Seeing how his lack of ambition was holding him back, however, just spurred me on to work harder and harder myself, both on the house, on my family and on my own future career.

When he arrived back on site later that afternoon we sat on a brick wall and I began apologizing for getting annoyed with him because I knew I'd been wrong to lose my temper. I was trying to explain that he could have a better life if only he chose to work at it, that success in any part of life is always hard work and that the rewards are there if you aim for them, but then my mouth suddenly overtook my mind and I blurted out the news that I had been unsuccessfully trying to find a way to introduce into the conversation for weeks.

'I've written a book,' I told him, my head down to avoid eye contact. 'It's going to be published in a few months' time.'

'Yeah?' He was obviously surprised and I could see his mind working as I looked up to gauge his reaction. 'What's it about then?'

'It's about my childhood mainly, and about the way Gloria and Dennis treated us,' I went on. 'I haven't said much about the rest of you, but I have put in a scene about that time you were in the bedroom with that man and I came in.'

I was nervous about whether he would want the

whole world knowing about the man who had abused him as a child, even though it wasn't his fault. I could see he was concentrating on what I was saying, taking it all in.

'I've just said that you were sitting on the bed together and he had your trousers down.'

I was unsure, especially not having seen him for so long, how he would react to me writing about such a personal incident. I'd kept putting off telling all of them about the book because I didn't know what I would do if any of my family objected strongly to my story being published at this late stage in the process.

'You could have written a hell of a lot more,' he said eventually, and I heaved a sigh of relief.

'I know I could,' I said, 'but I think readers will get the message.'

'No, I mean you could have written so much more about Gloria as well.'

'I could have, but I didn't want to be a neg-head. I've tried to make the book uplifting.'

As we sat on the wall in the sun, listening to Mark working away inside on his own, we became thoughtful. Both our minds were going back fifteen years or more.

'The trouble is though,' I said, 'I'm having real prob-lems with visions, scenes and smells from the past. I sometimes wake at night in a cold sweat or just think about them during the day. I can't seem to get the past out of my head. They did some sick shit.'

'Why do you think I've been in hospital?' he asked, breaking the silence as our feet swayed off the ground like two small boys.

'I don't know what you mean.'

He rolled his sleeve up and unwrapped the surgical dressing to show me the scar where the plate had recently been taken out.

'I had to have the plate put in because Gloria pushed me off a bike and I fell under a car,' he said. 'After that I was taken into care, and because of other stuff Gloria was banned from coming within a mile of me.'

I listened as he talked about his memories of childhood, which still seemed raw and painful for him. I realized now why he hadn't been there when I'd gone back for family visits during my time in the children's home. He'd been sent away to a care home in Wales, but no one ever told me any details. It seemed normal in our family.

'Social Services looked after me in care homes and foster homes until I was twenty-one,' he explained. 'Then I had to fend for myself, but I didn't know what to do.'

As he talked I realized why Robert was holding himself back in life. He knew the system had let him down; he knew that they should have done more for him and he was able to blame them for everything that subsequently went wrong in his life. It was then that I saw the biggest difference between us. I believed that if I sat at home and blamed all those people who had let me down in the past, I would be letting them win and I would never be able to move on. Instead I'd chosen to say, 'Fuck 'em! They're not going to ruin the rest of my life like they did the beginning. I'm not going to let them drag me down.'

I understood how he felt, especially with regard to

Gloria and Dennis still haunting me – it was sometimes as though they were standing over me – but I was determined to put it behind me. He wasn't choosing to do that and I could see this was the biggest thing holding him back. He couldn't stop blaming the authorities for letting him down. He was bitter and angry about the past and how he had been treated. His fantasies and exaggerations were just his way of living his dreams and escaping his past. The difference was I wanted to turn my dreams into reality and was making plans to move on and forget the past.

'Robert,' I said, 'you can't keep blaming everyone else and thinking of the past. I don't see Gloria as my mother; I just think of her as someone I knew, but not very well. Maybe that makes me seem cold, but I refuse to let any of them – Gloria, Dennis, the Social Services and the others – ruin my life. I only have one life. It's short enough as it is and I'm not going to waste any more of it.'

Robert went on to explain that after coming out of care with no idea how to look after himself, it wasn't long before he found himself on the streets, with no way of getting his life together. I remembered that feeling very well from when I left school and my foster parents and tried to make my way in an adult world that didn't seem to want to give me a break, having no food, no rent money or any way of getting on to the ladder. At one stage he'd got himself a flat, but then he'd let it go, through carelessness as much as anything. It seemed he wanted to be free of all ties and responsibilities. He didn't seem equipped or to even want to take on any of the pressures of normal life, like paying a bill or making a plan or saving money. It was easy to see how he might have got like that with only the examples of Gloria and Dennis to learn from. Listening to him I saw how my life could have easily gone the same way as his if I'd been just a little different or had fewer lucky breaks. But I made my breaks happen through sheer hard work and having the balls to take some risks and move on. I really wanted him to understand that he could do the same if he chose to. But I knew, as I did with my other brother and sisters, that I have always been different from them. At a very early age I used to get out the house to work, beg or just steal some food for them to eat. It came to me naturally. I don't know how, it just did.

I turned to face him and could see that he was getting upset by our conversation. I put my arm round his shoulders in an attempt to comfort him. It was clear from the way he sat, cold and rigid, that he wasn't used to the affection and didn't know how to react. There was nothing I could say to make the painful memories go away for him. We went back into the house a short while afterwards and carried on working, which seemed like a better thing to do than wallowing in the past. That night the three of us went out for a curry and got completely plastered, avoiding all mention of our parents or our childhoods. It was clear both Robert and I didn't like talking about our past, preferring to lock the painful memories away. After that brief moment of discovering how similar our experiences had been, and how differently we had reacted to them, it was time to move forward again on our separate paths.

When the house was nearly finished I helped Robert fill out some forms to apply for a council flat, but something else came up in his life and it wasn't long before he was back on the road again, searching for love or friendship or whatever it was he craved, living the sort of life he didn't seem to be able to give up. I was coming to the realization that he was probably too much of a free spirit to ever be able to put down roots. I know he'll turn up in our lives again one day, when he feels like it, and I will always be pleased to see him. We've come a long way together, even though we've been apart for almost all our lives. I was sad to see him go, but there was nothing I could do to stop him.

Having told Robert about the book I knew I had to tell the others quickly, in case they heard from someone else and thought that I was deliberately holding out on them. I know how nervous I would be feeling if I heard that one of them was writing a book about the family. I would definitely want to be told what was going to be said. I talked to my sisters first, knowing that my brother, Wayne, was still in touch with Gloria and feeling unsure about how either of them would react to the news that the world was going to be told about the suffering she inflicted on her children. It wasn't that I cared about confronting her with my stories of what she did to me as a child; it was just that I wanted my other brother and sisters to know first.

The grapevine worked quicker than I could, twisting the news like a game of Chinese whispers and Wayne heard that I'd said something derogatory about him in the story before I had a chance to talk to him, which I certainly hadn't, and he phoned me up in anger. When I explained exactly what I had said he calmed down. I promised to send him an advance copy as soon as I had one, so he could see for himself what I'd written.

When two of my sisters heard what I was doing, it opened the floodgates of their own memories and they started telling me things that they had been so careful to avoid thinking about for so many years. Like Robert, two of them came out with horror stories of their own about other attacks they'd suffered, some of which I had witnessed as a child and many of which I'd known nothing about because they'd happened at times when I was away from home. They told me of beatings with sticks and belt buckles, and of crockery being thrown at their heads. By then it was too late to add anything else to the book, and I didn't want to anyway. The readers were going to get enough of an idea of what life in the Lewis family was like from what I had told them. They didn't need to know every dreadful detail of what went on in that house during those years. All three of the girls said they had no objections to my story being told.

'Do you know,' the third one told me, wistfully, 'I don't remember anything before my thirteenth birthday.'

It seemed that her mind's way of coping with it all was to block it away completely. Whereas I had subconsciously built barriers against the pain for many years, her brain had simply chosen not to remember any of it, and now she could find no way in to the lost memories. We had all discovered different ways to put the past behind us and get on with our lives. With the exception of the sister who had lost her memories, once we started talking the rest of us remembered everything vividly, as if it had all happened yesterday, and as if the wounds still stung and the fear still chilled us. But we soon decided we didn't really want to talk about the past. We never had before and didn't really want to start bringing it all up now. The way we all dealt with it was to not think about it and just get on with life. They wished me all the best and it made me feel much better that they were supportive of the book. But as publication day drew nearer the past was about to repeat itself in the most sinister of ways.

9

History Repeating Itself

It was early one evening, soon after breaking the news of the forthcoming book to the family, that I received an hysterical phone call from one of my sisters. At first the shouting was so loud it could have been mistaken for Gloria, and I had to pull the phone away from my ear. I always experienced a terrible feeling of dread when I heard shouting voices, particularly women's. To me it was a reminder of the chaos of my past, hovering in the background, trying to engulf my new, happy, orderly life and destroy it, pulling me back to where I had started from. I kept quiet and listened intensely, waving at the children to go and play as I got up to find a more private room.

I couldn't make out what she was trying to say at first through the crying and raging. Eventually I managed to calm her down enough to make sense of the story she was telling me. My sister is a single mum with five kids and she had wanted to go out for the night with her friends. Having no one else to turn to she had asked Gloria to look after the children for that one night, and now they had come home with tales of how their grandmother had been hitting them. She said they had bruises to prove that their stories were true.

The news made me feel sick, as I was transported back once again through the years and imagined the nightmare the children must have been put through in those hours they were trapped with their screaming and violent grandmother. One of them told my sister that Gloria had beaten him with a wet towel. So many memories came rushing back. I could clearly picture the times I had seen my brothers and sisters being beaten until they collapsed. I remembered it happening to me and how terrifying it felt.

I would lose my breath while the blows rained down, struggling against the panic and pain, and then I would go limp, just like I had seen my brothers and sisters do. My head would feel light and I would collapse, my feet going from under me, trying to inhale but unable to do so out of sheer fright. Finally, with my face as white as chalk and my lips purple, some natural instinct would take over and I would draw huge amounts of air into my lungs. Then an almighty scream would roar out of me, driven by a mixture of pain and relief. But even then I wouldn't be able to convince Gloria that I was innocent of whatever the imagined crime might be and that I didn't deserve a beating. Witnessing my brothers and sisters being beaten was almost as frightening; watching their faces change colour, and their lips turn purple was always one of the most horrifying sights, especially if it happened to the girls. Sometimes I would shout out to stick up for them and be dragged into their place to take the punishment that Gloria had been intending for them. I still remembered times when I couldn't help them because of the agony I was in. It will always be painful for me to remember, to think of watching the beatings raining down and listening to their pleas for help, know-ing I was too weak to protect them.

Now I pictured the same thing happening all over again to my nephews and nieces when they thought they had just been left for the evening with their grandmother, this woman who had constantly been in my thoughts ever since writing the book. Thoughts of what she had done in the past and what she was doing today made me boil with anger.

My first thought was to go straight round to her flat and to show her what it felt like to be picked on by someone stronger than her, but reason prevailed, mainly because Jackie managed to calm me down before I did anything stupid. It was true that if I did something to Gloria that would merely have brought me down to her level, as if I had never learnt anything in all those years and would be perpetuating the violence even further. But I knew I had to do something.

'Give me her number,' I said to my sister, my legs shak-ing and my mind unable to believe that history could be repeating itself in this way. Hadn't this woman mellowed with age at all? I wondered. How could she do this? She must know what she was doing. My sister gave me the number of Gloria's mobile. 'A mobile?' I thought. 'Fuck me, she can't be living in the Dark Ages any more then.'

I dialled it straight away, my fingers trembling with fury. I knew that if she had been with me at that moment I would most probably have flown into an uncontrollable rage. I don't think anything would have stopped me and I don't know how it would have ended. I was even angrier to find myself talking about her as a woman when I didn't believe she deserved to be classed as one.

I didn't want time to think about what to say and I wasn't prepared to wait to let it settle. I was going to say whatever came out of my mouth without even thinking. It would be the first time I had spoken to Gloria since she came to our wedding several years before. She'd tried to make contact with us once or twice and I'd been told by the others that she still wanted to be part of our lives, but there was no way that would ever happen.

The phone only rang once before she picked it up, apparently excited to be receiving a call.

'It's Kevin,' I said in a stern voice that seemed to come naturally from the anger.

'All right, Kev?' she whimpered in a silly, girlish whine, immediately launching into a babbling diatribe about every problem in her life and every detail of her failing health.

'Listen!' I cut her short, speaking through gritted teeth. 'Why have you been smacking your own grandchildren?'

There was a long silence.

'I haven't,' she said eventually, without conviction. Her voice now quiet and submissive.

'Yes you have. I know you have. I've just been told. They've all got fucking bruises on them. What the fuck are you doing?'

My voice must have sounded venomous. I couldn't control it. So much hatred and anger was struggling to get out past the barriers of self-control.

There was another long silence, which I was determined not to break. My breathing was heavy and turning into panting under the stress of challenging Gloria. I pictured again the room with glass between us, but this time I was smashing it down to confront her instead of the other way round. All I could hear down the phone was the background sound of the television as she gathered her thoughts. I kept silent, trying to calm my breathing. I wasn't going to let her off the hook of answering. I was expecting the line to go dead but it didn't. If it had I would have gone round in person to have it out with her. I was so furious. The thought of history repeating itself was the final straw. Then a quiet little voice came back on the line, like an apologetic child trying to get back into favour after being told off.

'I only tapped them.'

'I know what your "taps" are like,' I said, my teeth still gritted. 'Leave them alone.' I spoke in a slow, pronounced way, wanting every word to sink into her head. She didn't reply and I had a feeling she genuinely thought she'd done nothing wrong. She actually believed that it was normal for adults to beat children up if they annoyed them.

It felt as if she was startled into silence at the discovery that I remembered the things she had done to me as a child. Maybe she thought that all children forget what has happened to them, as my sister had. Maybe she thought we all had fond memories of life with her and Dennis. Or maybe she knew exactly what she had done and what scars I was carrying because of her.

I'd heard rumours now and then that she was still up to her old tricks, but it was never spoken about openly. None of my sisters had ever come to me to explain exactly what was going on; they would just make generalized complaints about what had or hadn't happened.

Because I was always keen to distance myself from anything to do with her, I had never pressed them for details. For the first time someone had now told me exactly what had taken place. She couldn't lie her way out of this one, or pretend not to know what I was talking about. I could no longer kid myself that everything was all right and in the past, that she was a spent force and no longer a danger to anyone. I had finally got to hear what she was up to. It was as if I'd caught her unawares by producing evidence of her crimes, crimes that she professed to believe she hadn't committed. When actually confronted she had nothing else to say and no reason she could put forward to justify her actions.

As I slammed the phone down I was still shaking, every memory of what it had felt like to be at her mercy coming rushing back. I couldn't believe that she was still picking on people weaker than herself, like the playground bully who just can't resist taking one more punch at a victim who can't defend themselves. It amazed me that this woman was still so filled with anger and spite. Hearing that she was still hurting children banished any concerns I might have had about how she would feel when *The Kid* was published. There was no longer a shred of doubt in my mind; the world needed to know what she was like. She hadn't changed or mended any of her ways with the years. She was as violent and dangerous to children as she had always been and I was the only one with the power to stop her. It felt good to finally be able to stand up to her. I had tried so many times as a child to defend my brothers and sisters, or most of the time to defend myself. The difference now though was that I was bigger and stronger than her and she knew it. Like any bully she was reluctant to pick a fight she might lose.

A couple of minutes later the phone rang again and I picked it up with a trembling hand, taking a deep breath, still trying to recover from the anger that had exploded in my head and the verbal tirade that had poured from my mouth, leaving my whole body shaking. Gloria's voice came screeching down the line; before I'd even put the phone to my ear she was crying and yelling, swearing about how she was going to kill herself and a hundred other things about herself and the harm she was going to do. She'd had time to gather her thoughts and every one of them was bitter, angry and self-pitying. This was the Gloria I remembered and I had to hold the phone away from my ear once more, allowing the terrible voice out into the air. She'd recovered from the shock of having her bluff called and was now back on her old fighting form.

'Nobody loves me,' she wailed. 'Nobody wants to know what I'm doing. I'm just going to kill myself.'

She eventually fell quiet, as if she had exhausted herself, waiting for my reaction to what was supposed to be shocking news; no doubt frustrated at not being able to get a hold of me as she did when I was a child and shake me, bite me or beat me. Over the background sound of the television I could hear her constantly puffing away, all her frustrations being taken out on her fag.

My voice, when it eventually came must have sounded cold, as if every emotion had finally been drained from me. 'Why don't you?' I said.

She stayed silent for a moment longer.

'All right then,' she snarled, once she realized I wasn't going to retract my words, 'I fucking will.'

The phone line went dead. I look a lungful of air, trying to clear my head and contemplating what I had just said to my own mother. I kept the phone near me just in case she called again. I didn't want Jackie or the children picking up her call.

Any feelings of guilt I'd been harbouring about writing the book had vanished. Nothing had changed. Gloria had not mended her ways. Just because she was older now did not mean that the past should be buried. She was behaving in exactly the same ways she always had and she had to be stopped. People had to know the truth so that children would not be allowed near her.

Even months later I did not regret those terrible words. Whether it was a child or a puppy she would treat it the same, beating it into submission and breaking its spirit just for the pleasure of bending it to her will. When I spoke to my other two sisters about what had happened they both confessed that they had stopped taking their children to visit Gloria in the past, when she was abusive to them. They must have been dropping hints to me all the time and I had been choosing to ignore them, not feeling able to cope with the thought of confronting Gloria. Writing the book, however, had cleared up a lot of things in my mind and I was no longer willing to let her intimidate me in any way. I was now strong enough to lay down the law. I had to be or the cycle was never going to be broken.

My sisters also told me that if they saw Gloria in Croydon she would simply ignore them, only making contact when she was on the scrounge. It didn't seem as if she was doing anything to redeem herself with any of her children. She wanted their company, but only on her terms and only if they gave her money for fags or treats, like a child that needed to be bribed in order to be good.

People in authority might try to convince themselves that the bad old days of child abuse have gone and that the sort of things that happened to me would never be allowed to happen to a child these days, but they're kidding themselves. The same things were still happening with the same people in the same family. I couldn't bear the thought that history was repeating itself. I had really intended my warning to shock Gloria into realizing that what she had done was wrong, but the indignant hysteria of her response suggested that I still hadn't got through to her. I called my sister back and told her I'd spoken to our mother and if she needed any more help in future to just give me a call.

Later that evening, once the kids were in bed, I told Jackie what had happened. She knew something was wrong, having heard me shouting down the phone, and tried to calm me down as a quietness fell over the house once I'd hung up. Having just read about Gloria and what she did to her children, Jackie wasn't that surprised by the news that she was doing the same to her grand-children. Once I'd had time to calm down and think about it, I have to admit I wasn't that surprised either. I suppose I was just hoping that she'd got better with the years. I cried that night, asking myself over and over again why she was still able to torment me so. Little did I know that things were about to become far worse.

10

Going to Extremes

Whatever monsters might be re-emerging from my past, I was still determined that my family life with Jackie and the kids would continue to be as good as we could possibly make it. Having worked so hard to get the house into a good condition, and at the same time working late into the night on my film script, outlining my first novel and trying to find a way to get into the film business, it was time to have some treats. Moving back into a home of our own, after more than a year in rented accommodation, felt great. We felt we were safe and secure once more as a family.

Jackie knows that I've always loved the odd adrenalin rush. Perhaps it's a hangover from my childhood when high, constant doses of adrenalin were the norm, brought on by the stresses of family relationships rather than the experience of extreme sports. As anyone who has read *The Kid* will know, I'm always tempted to try anything that gives me that familiar tingling of excitement and danger. So, as a birthday present, Jackie gave me a couple of vouchers. The first was for a flight on a jet aircraft. It was something I had always wanted to do and I'd told Jackie of my dream one evening when we were watching Jeremy Clarkson together on television.

Clarkson was lucky enough to be passenger in an F14 fighter jet while it was being taken through its paces in America. The other voucher was for an introductory day playing polo.

My interest in polo had been triggered completely accidentally one day when I was driving along a country lane on the way to visit friends and saw a brightly coloured helmet and stick bobbing up and down behind a hedge. Always curious about new things I pulled the car over and got out to watch. There in the field were three or four people galloping around on horses, practising their polo. They looked so alive and so elegant; their horses (or, as I soon learned to say, polo ponies) were so controlled as their riders dribbled the ball and then took a full swing at it. The ball, which was only about three inches in diameter, was then struck squarely and would fly halfway up the field. The whole scene was so beautiful, like a snapshot that stays in your memory for ever. I'd heard of polo of course, but to see it happening in front of my own eyes transfixed me.

'Now that,' I thought as I watched them charging around, turning at the last minute and stroking the ball, which seemed to then fly for ever, 'is a bit of me.'

I stood there watching for what seemed like ages before getting back in the car and continuing my journey. All day I couldn't get the image of those men and their ponies out of my head. From that tiny taste I was as hooked as any junkie could be and I knew then that this was a game for me.

When I got home that evening I was still bubbling

with enthusiasm about the idea of playing polo and followed Jackie around the house like a small child, excitedly telling her every detail of what I'd seen and explaining how much I wanted to try it for myself.

'Just one problem,' she said, when I eventually let her get a word in.

'What's that?' I demanded, unable to see a single reason why I couldn't become an instant polo player.

'You can't ride.'

Bollocks to that, I thought, but said nothing.

It was true that I'd only ever sat on a horse once in my life, and on that occasion I hadn't done anything more than plod gently along on top of an old nag which had frankly seen better days. But I was sure I would be able to find my way round what I thought was such a minor obstacle. I brushed it aside as a mere detail that could quickly be rectified. I don't know if Jackie had as much faith in my abilities to learn a new skill overnight as I did, or whether she just wanted to show me the error of my ways, but it was soon after that that she bought me the day out at polo.

We decided, or should I say I decided, that we would take a weekend together to use both these vouchers. Jackie's mum agreed to look after the kids for the weekend and I booked to do the flight on a Dolphin L29 fighter jet on the Saturday and the polo on the Sunday. As compensation to Jackie for having to sit around watching me as I indulged myself, I agreed to go with her to Bluewater shopping centre after the flight. Even though I admit I'm a selfish shopper and find trailing around after Jackie as she wanders back and forth deliberating over every single purchase almost unbearable, I could see that I was still getting the best of the deal by a long way.

I was looking forward to my weekend full of adventure with mounting excitement as it approached and on the day of the flight I leapt out of bed eager with anticipation. I got up, dressed, and was ready to get out of the door within half an hour, hurrying poor Jackie along all the way out the house and into the car. I think her eyes eventually opened as I slammed the car door and headed down to Marsden Airport in Kent. It was a beautiful sunny morning and the air was crisp and fresh, with only a scattering of clouds in the sky. A perfect day for flying, I thought, as if I spent my life in the air and knew all about it. Jackie packed the video camera so that every second of my airborne adventure would be captured for posterity.

'I hope you enjoy this,' she said as we drove down. 'I hope you don't get sick.'

I suddenly remembered watching Jeremy Clarkson being thrown about on the F14 fighter jet, and the internal cameras filming him being ill over and over again. Wimp, I had thought. It had never occurred to me that such a thing would happen to me and I was confident nothing was going to spoil my day.

We arrived in plenty of time, with Jackie repeatedly pointing out that she could have had an extra hour in bed, and I was introduced to my pilot, Gary, who owned the Dolphin L29 two-seater jet plane and who made his living by providing thrills for adrenalin junkies like me. He was all kitted out in his flying gear and looking the business. My pulse was beginning to thump as I was taken to change into my co-pilot's gear, a green flying suit and helmet, and I could feel the tension of excitement building in my stomach. The pilot's wife was handling all the administration details and there were forms for me to sign and procedures to go through, listing minor details like, 'If you have to eject that's not our responsibility' – you know the kind of stuff.

'Well, enjoy your flight, Kevin,' she said, once the forms were signed. 'Don't forget, if you feel ill there's a sick bag on the right-hand side of the cockpit.'

I ignored the idea once again. It wasn't even going to enter my mind. I wanted to get on and enjoy this rush of adrenalin and I definitely wasn't going to do a 'Jeremy'. But she carried on, 'If you throw up in the plane, you'll have to clean it up yourself and there'll be a fifty-pound fine, so please use the bag.' No way was I going to do anything so pathetic. I'll leave that for Clarkson, I thought.

Gary then came back in to escort me to the plane and we both strode out on to the tarmac. The plane looked huge and I was getting more and more excited as we got closer and closer to this magnificent beast. I momentarily forgot who I was as we drew close to the jet, having visions of Tom Cruise in *Top Gun*, but I managed to get a grip and come back to reality before calling my pilot 'Iceman'. It was a great feeling; I was finally doing something I'd always dreamed of.

Gary walked me around the single-engine jet explaining things to me as he did his pre-flight checks.

'So, Kevin,' he said, 'what would you like to do? We could do some acrobatics or some low-level flying.'

'Oh, you know,' I replied, trying to sound casual, 'let's just get up there and throw it about a bit.'

It didn't occur to me that this might be the worst thing imaginable to say to a pilot who wants nothing more than to relieve the boredom of normal flying with a bit of extra daredevilry. I'd just given him permission to do whatever he liked – a huge mistake!

I climbed into my seat behind his with my back to the engine and he strapped me in tightly, showing me how the ejector seat worked and telling me the commands he would give in an emergency. He then pointed over my right shoulder to the sick bags at the side of the cockpit, in case they were needed. Looking back now I have to admit he did have a slightly sinister smile on his face. I just grinned confidently back, much like a turkey enjoying a pre-Christmas pep talk from Bernard Matthews.

Once in the plane Gary gunned the engine with a mighty roar that throbbed through my whole body, making every hair on my skin rise with anticipation and my legs tingle with excitement. Jackie was filming every moment, and I waved from behind the pilot with a grin that could have lifted the plane on its own.

As we taxied off I looked around the cockpit. There were buttons and knobs everywhere in front of me and down the sides. All of them must have had a purpose, but not for me. The only thing I had to decide was where to rest my arms and hands to be sure I didn't touch anything by mistake. I decided to put them on my legs. This was something I'd wanted to do for so long and I was loving every moment. That was of course until we got into the air.

Gary, my trusted pilot, gave me a few instructions

over the headphones as we taxied out on to the runway, his voice surrounded with static, just like in the movies. While he communicated with the tower we remained stationary, waiting for our moment to take off. Then the engine erupted and roared into action. It grew louder and louder, making my whole body tingle with excitement. Gary must have let go of the brakes because we raced along the runway and, with another huge roar, we took off. We were up above the sea within seconds, looking down on a cargo ship below, the water as still as a millpond, reflecting the dazzling sun.

As we climbed high up into a safe position we made smalltalk over the radio. Then Gary's tone changed and he said in a serious voice, 'OK, Kevin, first we need to see if you can take some Gs.'

Before I could answer he'd flipped the plane over to the right and we plummeted through the skies, soaring up at the last moment to complete a full loop.

'Fuuuuuuuuuuuuuuuuuuuck!' Suddenly it felt like my arse was being sucked out the back of the plane. My hands were all over the place and I grabbed on to the seat belt, clinging on as if my life depended on it. He then brought the jet back to its original position before flipping it and doing a loop to the left, with the same result. My neck was so tense from fighting with the G-forces that I had to rest it on the back of the seat.

Oh, shit, I thought, as he kept throwing the jet about like a child running around the house with a toy plane. Where did they say those sick bags were?

I wasn't going to ask Gary, who seemed to be relishing the freedom I'd given him to hurl his plane around the skies. My eyes were frantically scanning the cockpit. I looked down and there they were, three wax paper bags. I grabbed one and was instantly sick. 'Oh, bollocks,' I said to myself, my eyes beginning to feel as giddy as a drunk and my stomach heaving.

'You all right, Kevin?' he asked, but didn't wait for an answer before heading off into a series of different manoeuvres, each one more stomach-churning than the last. We went up in a vertical line, the jet blasting us through the sky, resting at the top for a few seconds before heading straight down with such force that the smile was put back on my face by the G-force. Gary then banked it to the right then the left – you name it he did it. Had you been listening in all you would have heard coming from the back of the jet was 'fuck', 'shit', 'bollocks', 'fuck'.

My main concern now was how not to spill the contents of the sick bag and what to do if it split as I went back to use it again and again. I couldn't believe that I'd been ill within only a few minutes of being up in the air and I still had another painful twenty-eight minutes to endure. I couldn't reach for a new bag because I now didn't know where to put the full one.

'Are you OK, Kevin?' he asked again.

'Bastard!' I replied, and he just laughed. Sadist, I thought to myself.

Eventually he took mercy on me. 'Kevin, would you like to take control? It'll help you focus your mind.' He obviously knew I'd been ill. 'Also, try looking ahead.' He could have told me that at the beginning, I thought.

As I tried to focus on what was outside the plane rather than on what was inside my stomach, I wondered what to look at. I could barely see out of the cockpit as I grasped the flight stick, holding the sick bag in my other hand as I took control.

'I have control,' I said, like I knew what I was doing.

'You have control,' he confirmed, and there I was, flying a jet.

'Move the stick about a bit,' Gary told me, but I had no idea how responsive the jet would be.

I pushed it forward and we dropped so hard and fast that all I said was, 'You have control.' In fact I think I might have screamed it rather than said it, sounding a bit like Jackie when she comes across a spider unexpectedly.

Gary instantly took over. 'Have you had enough acrobatics?' he said.

'I'd say so.'

I admitted that I couldn't take any more, but was determined not to go back early. We then came down to do some low-level flying between the cargo ships, which had looked so close together from high up in the skies, but now seemed miles apart as we sped over the calm, sparkling waters of the open sea that looked to be no more than a hundred feet below our wings.

By this time I felt so ill and weak I couldn't even respond when he spoke to me. Returning to the airport he performed one last loop before coming in to land and then threw open the canopy so I could take some welcome gulps of fresh air. I could see Jackie and the pilot's wife coming over towards us, with Jackie filming as she walked, and there was nothing else I could do but hold my unbroken sick bag triumphantly in the air like a trophy. I got out and fell to the ground, knackered, tired and feeling very queasy. The tarmac was moving uncomfortably beneath my feet.

'Full respect to Jeremy Clarkson,' I murmured weakly.

'What?' the three of them said.

'Nothing,' I replied, not having the energy to explain.

Gary gave me a pat on the back and strode inside as Jackie knelt down beside me.

'Are you all right?' she asked. Her voice sounded concerned, but I was sure I could detect a smirk on her face.

That afternoon I did my very best to keep my side of the bargain with Jackie, trailing along behind her at the shopping centre from one noisy, stuffy, overcrowded shop to the next with my insides wobbling precariously around, wondering if I would ever be able to face the sight of food and drink again. Eventually I couldn't take another step, my face was pale and all I could think to myself was, serves you right. By four o'clock I was back home lying on the sofa, still feeling green, and our plan for going out to dinner that evening had to be scrapped.

It's great to have an opportunity to live out your childhood dreams because I now know that I never want to go near a jet fighter ever again, even if I live to be a hundred. I went to bed early that evening in order to get a good night's rest before my next adventure. At least all I'd have to do there was hit a ball, I thought.

I was still feeling rough when I woke up the following morning and set off for my day's polo experience. I'd been looking forward to the flying but having discovered what that involved I had become quietly confident that I would enjoy the polo more. As we arrived, however, the reality of the situation began to dawn on me, reminding me that I'd never actually ridden a horse properly before. I pushed my doubts to the back of my mind, telling myself that anything must be possible after that jet ride.

Even as the day got under way I wasn't sure if I was in the right place. The men I'd watched playing in the field by the roadside had impressed me with their speed and ferocity and the control they had over their ponies. It seemed a long way from standing on a milk crate on a Sunday morning in the middle of winter, in a line with nine other novices, swiping at a ball with a mallet. After a couple of hours of standing on the milk crates they then explained the basics of the game and it was time to get on to my first polo pony.

When the instructors brought the ponies out they looked extremely bored, nothing like the energetic animals I'd watched that day over the hedge. I realized that no one in their right mind would allow a bunch of beginners to use their finest string of polo ponies and that this might be a good place to start. An old grey pony was brought up to me. It remained stationary and quiet and seemed well behaved – just what I needed. I stood on top of the milk crate and clambered on to the pony as it stood, solid and patient. No problem. I then tried to get it started. I could almost feel it sighing with resignation beneath me as I flipped my arms like a chicken and my legs pumped back and forth as if I was pedalling a pushbike.

This animal was obviously so used to dealing with inexperienced idiots like me it knew that all it had to do was walk to where the ball was, stop and wait for me to hit it and I would be happy. So there I was in the arena, swinging the mallet, missing the ball and now and then hitting the pony's legs, then looking round to see if anyone had seen me do it. I caught Jackie's eye and we exchanged grins. On the odd occasion that I did hit the ball the little grey would stroll on to wherever it had landed and wait patiently until I managed to repeat the exercise.

It was a pleasant way to spend a day, but hardly enough to get the adrenalin pumping through the veins. I knew I wanted more. After my group lesson and being told my day had come to an end, I got off the pony feeling as though I was walking like a frog. I hopped out of the arena and Jackie and I stayed to watch the game that was on after us. The riders suddenly became competitive and I felt the same rush of excitement as when I first saw the men practising in the field. I loved the atmosphere of the place, the pounding of the hoofs and the scent of the horses. I couldn't wait to get out on to the field and try it out for myself on a pony that was actually willing to move. But first I had to learn to play the game properly.

Nothing that happened that day had put me off trying the game, in fact it cemented in my mind the idea that this was something I really wanted to do, although I could see that I would have to get a lot more training before I could even think about going out to play properly. There was also no getting away from the fact that I was going to have to learn to ride as well. It wasn't that I was afraid of horses, exactly, I just didn't know what to expect from them and consequently wasn't confident around them. They seemed to be a lot bigger than me and somewhat unpredictable, especially with my chicken arms and bicycle legs.

All the way home I was still brimming with enthusiasm. My first taste of polo had whetted my appetite and I wanted more. The next day I rang the polo club and asked about going to the next stage. They advised having some individual coaching with one of their professionals. They booked me in for lessons the following week with a professional polo player by the name of Martin.

'So,' he said when I turned up on the first day, 'how many times have you ridden?'

'Oh,' I searched the air for an appropriate number, as if there had been so many times it was hard to remember, anxious not to be given the same donkey they'd put me on before, but also not wanting something that would be way out of my league. 'Twelve, fifteen times,' I said, guessing that this figure would at least get me off the starting block.

Martin nodded as if that was enough information for him. He lent me some polo boots, a polo stick, a whip and, most importantly, a helmet and we headed over to the arena once more where a suitable pony for my fabricated experience was awaiting my arrival. As I got closer I could see that it was a lot leaner, younger and more powerful than the grey I first tried. I strode over to mount it in what I hoped would seem like an experienced manner, both to Martin and to the pony itself. I knew it was important to show the animal who was boss from the start. It was only when I took hold of the saddle and slotted one foot into a stirrup that I realized I couldn't get on. I didn't appear to have any of the necessary muscles to simultaneously jump and throw my leg over in the casual way the professionals did. I might be fit enough to refurbish a house or run a few miles, but I still couldn't make my limbs perform this simple task. I scanned the area for the milk crate I'd used previously but it was nowhere to be found. I couldn't allow myself to be beaten at this early stage and eventually, with a great deal of huffing and puffing, I managed to hoist myself on board with Martin holding the saddle firmly down on the other side to counterbalance me. I thought at one point that the pony was going to fall on top of me as I struggled to get on. Eventually, there I was on top of this beautiful-looking polo pony, feeling proud of myself simply to have mounted it; but it was now far too late to convince the animal that I was master of the situation.

I don't know what I did to indicate to him that he should take off at full speed the moment I was on top of him, but he did, and before I knew it I was back on the ground again, exactly where I'd started, except this time I was on my backside. Martin patiently told me what I had done wrong.

'You kicked into his belly and let the reins loosen at the same time,' he said. 'Settle into the saddle, keep your legs away from his belly. Think of him as a Ferrari. He's very powerful and very responsive and you must handle him with care, as you would the car, otherwise you may be giving him signals without even knowing it.

'Let's try that again,' he suggested politely as I stood up, swearing under my breath as I dusted myself off.

Any hope of recovering my dignity vanished when

exactly the same thing happened a second time and Martin realized he was going to have to change the pony and give me a few tips just to keep me mounted long enough to learn something about the game. Eventually I had to admit that I might have got my calculations wrong and perhaps I hadn't ridden quite as many times as I'd first thought.

'I think I may have forgotten quite a lot of what I was taught,' I blathered. 'It was so long ago.'

I got the impression he knew what I was saying and didn't seem surprised, just chuckling as if he had known all along.

The pony, who I dare say was also still chuckling to himself at having called my bluff so easily, was taken away and another one was brought out. My heart sank as I recognized the same animal I'd had on the first day, but I was hardly in a position to protest and actually I was quite looking forward to not falling off for a while. Martin patiently explained once more:

'Keep your legs away from its belly. Just grip on with your knees.'

I'd never used these inner-leg muscles before and it wasn't long before my legs were burning from the strain of trying to grip with my knees and inner thighs. The pain didn't last long and I was soon sitting comfortably, walking and slowly cantering around the arena. My bottom bumping out of sequence with the pony made my whole body shake. But when I did manage to hit the ball from time to time a smile would spread across my face just long enough to register my delight before my body was bouncing around the arena once more.

The more I learnt about the game the more I realized how much skill was needed in order to succeed. I was determined to become good at it, but I knew that wouldn't happen overnight, especially with my lack of riding skills. Hitting a ball with a mallet in your right hand while controlling a horse with your left is not easy. I realized that this was going to be a very dangerous sport if I didn't learn to ride properly and so, to begin with, my lessons consisted mainly of riding, with the last twenty minutes being stick and ball skills around the arena. From there I began playing in 'practice chukkas'.

Just to explain to those of you who aren't familiar with the game, polo teams are made up of four players and a game consists of either four, five or six seven-minute periods, depending on the level of polo being played. Each period of play is called a 'chukka'. At the end of a chukka the first bell rings and an additional thirty seconds is given until the ball goes out of play or a foul is committed. Once the second bell has rung the players stop play immediately and there is a three-minute interval during which the players leave the ground and the ponies are changed. Each player is handicapped annually and a handicap can range from minus two to ten. The figures refer to the player's value to the team. Being a beginner I was a 'minus-two' player and at the other end of the scale there are only a handful of ten-goal players in the world. Each team is built from scratch, with the sum of the players' handicaps being added together to make sure that teams are broadly similar in skill. So a four-goal competition is one in which the players' combined handicaps must not exceed four.

Every time a goal is scored the teams effectively change ends and have to try to score in the opposite goal. A player following in the line behind the ball he or she has just hit has the 'Right of Way' over everyone else on the field. It is the most important rule of polo and is there to prevent serious injury to both players and ponies. You can of course ride people off the line. Got it? I hope so.

Anyhow, the practice chukkas were designed to bring me in slowly to the game and, more importantly, to teach me the theory of who should be where and what not to do in order to avoid dangerous play. When you're galloping around a pitch at forty miles an hour with only a helmet to protect you, it's all too easy to seriously injure yourself or other players if you're not vigilant and careful.

The more I practised the less nervous I became around the ponies. I really began to feel affection for these gracious animals, finding myself able to get closer and enjoy them more. They seemed to be able to sense my growing confidence but I knew that if I wanted to play seriously I needed to buy my own ponies, and that riding them regularly would give me the extra level of confidence I needed to move forward with my game.

I spent hours watching, picking up hints just from seeing the professionals play. I wanted to play more but I couldn't since renting ponies was an expensive business and I had very limited funds. I knew that I would have to wait until the time was right for me to buy my first polo pony.

I spoke about it at great length many times with Jackie, who could see that it was something I was passionate about, even after my limited experience. We had a little bit of money in the bank left over from the advance I'd received for *The Kid* and she agreed to let me use it to purchase my first polo pony. We knew that you actually need a minimum of four ponies in order to play seriously, but one was enough for now and at least I knew it would get me started.

I'd heard through friends of a couple who were in the game and might be able to help me, so I went to meet them. They told me they knew of some good ponies in Argentina, the international home of polo. Since I had no other contacts in the polo world and wouldn't have known how to start going about buying a pony on my own in England, I agreed to let them buy one on my behalf. They knew the sort of thing I needed, something for a beginner with the ability to grow with me as my skills improved, and so made the buying decision for me.

Just before the start of the season, which runs from the end of April to the end of September, I took delivery of Mistico, a delicate and agile pony, jet black with a white stripe on the crown of its head. Mistico gradually lightened in colour through the summer like a chameleon. I'd acquired my first animal and I must say he looked magnificent. It felt brilliant. I was now looking forward to the season ahead, knowing that if I was going to improve at any reasonable rate I needed to find somewhere where I could go to play as often as possible. With that in mind I joined Knepp Castle Polo Club in West Sussex, about thirty minutes' drive from the house. I couldn't wait to get started.

A Bit of Pampering

The Kid was due to be published. Even though I was busily getting on with my new life, I once again found myself becoming apprehensive as memories and visions of my past began to reappear as publication day drew closer and closer. Before publication day I thought it would be a good idea for Jackie and me to spend some quality time together in order to calm us down. We were both tense with a mixture of excitement and nerves. Jackie isn't interested in anything to do with adrenalin rushes or fast-moving sports. Her idea of a really good day out is to relax at a health spa, somewhere where she can be a million miles away from the demands of the house and the children. She loves nothing better than to wander around in a luxurious dressing gown being pampered from head to toe. Since she was always so tolerant of my little enthusiasms I thought the least I could do was take her for a weekend at a health farm.

She was keen to show me how great it would be to relax and let go of my inhibitions a bit, and had booked me in for a batch of treatments like a massage and a seaweed wrap. Just the names of the treatments filled me with a strange foreboding. To start with I'm not very good at sitting still. I can't even stay in one room of my own house for more than an hour or two at a time without wanting to get up and move about. I was also unsure how I would feel about being touched by a stranger, even if they were a professional masseur. I dare say it all stems from my childhood.

Anyhow, the massage was the first thing on the weekend itinerary and I ventured cautiously into my allotted candlelit cubicle. I sat in my trunks on the long, funny-looking bed with a hole at one end and, after a while, a lady came in dressed in white. She told me her name, which I was too nervous to remember, and I told her mine and then she asked me to lie face down. She draped a towel over my trunks. Now I realized that the hole was there to stop me from suffocating.

It didn't start well. I couldn't stop chattering through the breathing hole, which was sticking to my cheeks making me sound as if I'd just had my teeth taken out. Then, as the woman put her warm soft hands on me, and started to oil me up with some sweet-smelling lotion, I began to feel deeply uncomfortable. I wanted to overcome the feelings and relax and so I stopped talking, which my cheeks were very happy about, and attempted to enjoy the experience like other people. I tried to force myself, but it was impossible. I lay there completely rigid, very awake and unable to relax. Whatever barriers against being touched by strangers had been built in my brain from my past weren't going to evaporate just because I wanted them to. I could tell I was going to end up feeling far worse at the finish of the session than I had when I first walked in.

'I'm so sorry,' I told the rather shocked woman, sitting

up and sliding off the table, 'it's nothing to do with you. I'm sure you're really good at this, but it's my first massage and I'm really not enjoying the experience.'

I escaped from the cubicle as quickly as I could, leaving the poor woman looking puzzled as I hurried to our room to get the gunge off my back.

The next thing Jackie had booked for us was the seaweed wrap. After the massage experience, she told me she thought this one would be right up my street, and was trying to convince me, unable to suppress the odd burst of giggles. What the hell was I about to put myself through? I wondered. We both arrived at the appointed place at the appointed time to be greeted by two people looking like nurses, dressed in all white, who led us into separate cubicles. Jackie smiled at me as I went into my room and I poked my tongue out at her before she was out of sight. I could hear her giggle as the door was closed behind me. Inside was another couch, but this time there was no hole in it. Instead there were layers of some sort of filmy material, which were hanging down from either side. The lady offered to take my dressing gown and handed me a pair of what looked like rubber incontinence pants. I warily placed them over my swimming shorts and was led to the waiting couch for my treatment.

I lay down on the plastic film and prepared myself for the experience, determined to do my best to see this one through to the end and enjoy it. The very polite lady who was going to be administering the treatment then came over with her pot of slimy green seaweed gunk, which absolutely stank. This didn't make me feel any more comfortable than I probably looked. She then smothered me in the foul-smelling paste from the neck downwards.

My skin felt like it was burning off me. My arms were down at my sides and, once she'd thoroughly basted me, she pulled the cling film round me, trussing me up like Tutankamun's mummy. As the heat built up inside the wrap she spread a layer of towels over it and finally what looked like tin foil on top of that.

I stayed very still and quiet and forced myself to just chill as the temperature inside my cocoon rose to what felt like combustible levels. The sweat was pouring off me as I lay there wondering if I was going to be able to last for the whole thirty-minute session. I knew Jackie was in the next cubicle and would be loving every minute of this, so I gritted my teeth and held on, waiting to feel the benefit.

'I'll be back in thirty minutes,' the lady said, when she'd finished preparing and wrapping me like Christmas dinner.

'But what do I do now?' I squeaked, trying in vain to keep my voice as relaxed as I could.

'Try closing your eyes and enjoying it,' she said, as if it was the most obvious thing in the world. She turned on some kind of rainforest music and quietly closed the door behind her. My eyes were shut and I was suddenly alone, simmering in my own private oven.

The minutes ticked slowly past and it wasn't long before I began to get the fidgets. Beads of sweat were trickling down from my brow, puddling in my eye sockets and then overflowing on to my nose, making it itch. Because I was unable to move my arms to scratch, the intensity of the itching increased and I started contorting my face into strange expressions to try to stop them. It didn't work. I tried to ignore the itching, thinking perhaps I could exert mind over matter, but it was hopeless, the need to scratch merely intensified. It was no good; I was going to have to do something about it.

Terrified of disturbing her careful wrapping, I inched my right hand slowly across my stomach, up over my chest towards the opening for my head. After what seemed like an age my fingers made it into the fresh air and, blessed relief, I was able to scratch my nose, leaving a blob of the smelly gunk on the end of it. Lost in the bliss of the moment I forgot myself and moved too far. I felt the tension of the wrapping go as the left side fell away. 'Oh shit,' I said.

Still moving in slow motion, while at the same time trying to blow the sweaty gunk away from my nose, I slid my other arm across my chest and attempted to pull the wrapping back round me, but the strain was too much, the overall cocoon had been weakened and I felt a blast of cool air as the right side fell away as well. 'Fuck!' I said.

I now had to employ both hands to try to re-wrap myself from inside the parcel before the woman returned and saw the mess I'd made of her handiwork, and I was also bloody freezing. Now that the wrap was off the outside air was getting to my hot skin and I was beginning to shiver with cold. The green slime was escaping over everything as I struggled to pull both sides back together. I must have struggled for fifteen minutes before the lady came in to check how I was getting on and saw her work strewn around the room in ruins.

'Get me out of here,' I ranted. 'I bloody hate this.'

'Aren't you enjoying it?' She looked dismayed as I sat up like the monster from the Black Lagoon, the seaweed falling all around me.

'No, I am not,' I said. 'I just want a shower to get rid of this smell.'

Once I was showered and fresh-smelling again I went to find myself a comfy bed by the pool and sat reading a book. Jackie came to sit with me a short while afterwards. I explained what had happened, but she'd already heard from the staff and we couldn't help laughing together. I decided that for the rest of the weekend I would leave the treatments to Jackie.

12

Published

As the moment of publication drew nearer I became more and more concerned about the path I'd chosen to follow. I kept seeing myself huddled into a corner with Gloria and Dennis hovering over me and I began withdrawing further inside my thoughts. I tried to prepare myself mentally for what was about to happen, but it all felt so personal; having the world reading about things I'd been keeping secret for so many years still left me feeling as naked as on the first visit to the publishers. My recollections of the past seemed as vivid and real today as they had all those years before, mainly because I now understood clearly what was going on, whereas as a child I would just put up with it. Everyone who read the book would now know the kind of degrading, embarrassing things that I went through as a child, as well as the things I'd got up to as a young adult.

The process of putting everything on paper was the first time in my life that I'd ever thought deeply about my early life and attempted to understand what had happened to me, rather than simply blocking it out and trying to fool myself into believing it had never happened. It was as if the truth had been festering unexamined and untreated in my head for years and, as well as worrying about how the public would react to finding out about it, I also had to come to terms with what I had written myself, which I didn't seem to be able to do.

I had to work out a way to handle the truth now that it was coming out into the open. I could no longer stick my head in the sand and hope it would all go away. These things really had happened and I needed to find a way to deal with them. If I didn't then I was afraid I was going to be going further and further back inside myself, which would affect my family, the three people I loved and felt most protective about.

People like Barbara and the publishers kept telling me that I had nothing to be embarrassed about or ashamed of, and I dare say in their eyes I didn't; but in mine I did because I went through it and now it seemed as though I was reliving the whole nightmare again, day after day. Because I wasn't sleeping well either, this was making me tired during the day and I often felt lethargic. Lying awake in the middle of the night was the worst time for my thoughts. I tried to break the cycle by taking some sleeping pills to help me sleep all through the night but this just made me even more dopey during the day, so I stopped. I knew there was no going back now and that was a frightening prospect as I didn't have control of the childhood thoughts which now seemed to be whirling around my head twenty-four seven. It was as if I'd started the ball rolling and I couldn't do anything to control where it went or when it would stop as it gathered momentum. I was beginning to fear that it might do some damage as it hurtled on its way.

I arrived home from taking one of the kids to school a few weeks before publication to find the post had been. My eyes were instantly drawn to the brown envelope. I just knew what it would contain. It was A4 in size with the Penguin logo shining out on the white address label, giving the game away. I deliberately opened the other post first, leaving the large envelope on the kitchen table while I made myself some toast, my eyes constantly being drawn back to it. In the end I couldn't put the moment off any longer. I sat at the table alone, Jackie having gone out, and I opened it. There it was, my first copy of *The Kid*. I looked all around the book, smelling and feeling it all over. I didn't read any of the words inside as I already knew what was in there. The team at Michael Joseph had obviously invested a lot of effort, and the photographer and designer had produced a stunning cover with a white background and a photograph of the back view of a small, bedraggled boy. My story was printed and published and about to be released to the public. Money had been invested, contracts had been signed and foreign rights were being sold to places as varied as Japan and Denmark. My life had become a product, part of the business cycle and in some respects I thought it would be easier to try to treat it that way.

The cover reminded me of being in that room playing with the train I'd acquired from a jumble sale, the music playing quietly from the Walkman that had been given to me by my teacher, Colin Smith, both of which I hid in my mattress during the day.

As I sat down and stared at it for a while, I wondered what Gloria and Dennis would say when they saw it.

Would they deny everything and call me a liar? Would they claim that none of it had ever happened? Only time would tell but, you know what, I really didn't care what they thought. Recent events had hardened me to that. What I did know was that the juggernaut was picking up speed and there was no way I could jump off now. All I could do was hang on tight and hope for the best. I placed the book gently back down on the kitchen table. I got myself a pen and wrote inside, *'To my darling Jackie, I mean every word, all my love, K.'* It instinctively seemed the right thing to do with the first copy.

The publishing team had invited me to London for the odd lunch during the previous few months and I would sit happily in restaurants in the midst of all these enthusiastic young ladies, listening to them talk of serialization deals with newspapers and interviews with the media. I tried not to think or tell them of how I was feeling about suddenly being exposed to the world, or confess that I was finding it hard to come to terms with what I had written, especially with the latest revelations about how Gloria was behaving now.

I received a call late one afternoon to tell me that a serialization deal had been agreed with the *Daily Mail*, which meant they would be printing extracts from the book just before publication. They didn't want to interview me, which I was slightly relieved about, but I was then booked up to do about five interviews with other newspapers and radio programmes after the serialization had appeared. In total the publicity was going to be spread over four weeks.

This was getting scary. I was working myself into a

panic and getting annoyed with myself for not being able to think calmly about my past without conjuring up hosts of demons. I tried to remember the good times, like my time at Yarborough children's home where I spent nearly two years away from the house. Then I thought of the day I was sent back home and pictured Uncle David bending down on his knees to say good-bye. I remembered getting out of the social worker's car and walking up the path to the family house once more, knowing that I didn't have any say in my own fate and that nobody would be asking if I wanted to go back. Stepping in front of the media felt as though I was walking out on stage dressed as Worzel Gummidge again. In agreeing to sell the book I'd taken on the responsibility for making it work in any way I could, no matter how apprehensive I might feel at the prospect of talking about my past to a stranger. Sometimes when I thought about it I would start to cry, feeling vulnerable and nervous in a world where everyone would be taking me at face value without knowing me. I was determined to go through with my end of the deal and do everything within my power to make the book a success. The only way I would be able to deal with it was to just keep my head high and not think about all the attention that might be coming my way.

One evening close to publication I looked at myself hard in the mirror. 'I agreed to do this,' I said, staring intensely into my own eyes. 'I was the one who opened the can of worms and I was quick enough to accept the advance money. No one forced me into it. I could always have said "No". Now I have to go through with it and in time I will show everyone that I can move away from my past and prove to them what I am capable of.'

As if that wasn't enough for me to focus on, other things were about to spiral out of control and history was about to repeat itself yet again.

13

Feeling Exposed

The serialization of *The Kid* came out in the *Daily Mail* as expected, just before the book was launched into the shops. The first morning it was out I got up just as the sun was rising, having lain awake thinking about it all through the night. I went to get the paper, not knowing quite what to expect or quite how I felt about it all. Although I understood that they would be printing extracts from the story, and despite the fact that I had posed for their photographer, I was still taken by surprise when I actually opened the paper on that first morning in the car before going home to show Jackie. There it was, the serialization of *The Kid* with a small picture of my adult face staring out at me, and one of the few pictures in existence of me as a child blown up on the opposite page for maximum impact. My eyes quickly scanned over it. My heart was racing. I was, I must admit, excited and nervous, but I knew I didn't want to read beyond lurid headlines:

TORTURED BY HIS OWN PARENTS

It's one of the most shocking stories you will ever read. This boy's parents beat him, bit him, crushed his fingers in a mangle and starved him until he ached with hunger. And the welfare workers who could have saved him just turned their backs.

It's one thing understanding intellectually that something is going to happen, quite another to experience it. I knew the story was coming and I knew they were bound to sensationalize it, but when I saw it there in black and white and realized that the millions of people who bought the paper that day would be seeing the same thing, I felt terrifyingly exposed and worried that people would feel sorry for me. The one reaction I dreaded the most. I could imagine how neighbours, acquaintances and friends who had known nothing about my past would be ringing one another and talking about it when they realized that it was about someone they knew. The only people I'd told were my brothers and sisters. Jackie had told her mother, but that was it. I imagined people who knew my brothers and sisters would be taking the paper to show them, if they hadn't seen it for themselves already. I wondered if anyone would have the courage to show it to Gloria and I imagined her screaming and banging once more against the glass panel, with me just continuing to draw, ignoring her. If she saw it, she would read me describing scenes that she must have hoped no one else would ever know about unless they were in the house at the time. All these questions and feelings were spinning through my mind as I tried to get them into some sort of order.

When I got home I showed Jackie the pages. We both knew what was contained in those columns of words and didn't need to go through it all again. We decided just to put the article away without reading it and get on with everything else we had planned to do with our day. I was determined to stay in control of my emotions, not knowing what sort of reaction I might expect from the outside world.

The day passed without any reaction. The calm was almost spooky. The next day they printed the second installment with a large picture of me as I look today and another dramatic headline.

My brutal parents beat me. Then I was drawn into a life of guns and violence. All I wanted to do was die . . . until one woman's love brought me hope.

'Bloody hell,' I said when I saw the picture. 'I look like Camp Freddie from *The Italian Job.*'

We laughed and put the paper away with the other one, getting on with our daily life once more. Nothing terrible had happened. The sky hadn't fallen in on us, so maybe this wasn't going to be so difficult after all.

The book might not yet have been launched, but the story certainly had. This picture was easily identifiable as being me and over the following few days I began to notice that strangers were recognizing me in the street. They didn't come up to me, but they would look twice, and maybe nudge someone to point me out. None of it was hostile, but it still made me want to pull back inside myself and hide my face. I was frightened of making eye contact with them in case they were able to see just how vulnerable I felt.

Jackie noticed that I was becoming increasingly jumpy and agitated as the date of the book launch loomed closer.

'Are you OK?' she asked one day, when I was feeling particularly sombre.

'It all feels a little weird,' I replied. She put her arms around me and I hid my face in her chest. She didn't know what to say, but her quiet support and love was enough to comfort me. She could understand now why I would wake early in the morning and come downstairs, unable to sleep, my thoughts driving me insane as I constantly churned over and over the past.

Then late one evening, a few days before publication, Jackie and I were getting ready to go to bed when the phone rang. It was one of those calls that I instinctively knew was wrong. I don't know how I knew that, I just did. I picked it up and it was one of my sisters. Jackie had already gone upstairs. My sister didn't bother to exchange any pleasantries.

'All you all right?' I asked, feeling a little too tired for a long conversation and wanting to get to bed.

She immediately explained that another of my sisters had had her five children taken into care. They had all been placed into a temporary foster home together. My stomach turned over in a horribly familiar way. I was now fully awake, all thoughts of settling down to sleep banished once more. I walked into the lounge and sat down, completely speechless. The news came completely out of the blue. I'd been talking to the sister in question just a few weeks before and she'd been telling me that everything was fine, but obviously it couldn't have been even then.

It was the same family of children who had been smacked by Gloria a few months before and I began to picture exactly what they must have been going through before the Social Services took them to safety. It seemed that it wasn't just Gloria who'd been giving them a hard time. I listened to everything my sister had to tell me and we agreed to speak again soon. I felt as if I was in a daze as I went upstairs and told Jackie what had happened. She was as shocked as me and obviously didn't know what to say or do either. I no longer felt like going to bed, knowing that I wouldn't be able to sleep, so I went back downstairs and sat alone on the sofa feeling numb with shock and sadness.

My mind went back and all I could think about was how long the kids had suffered before the authorities had decided things were so bad they had to step in. I could so easily imagine how frightening and unhappy their lives must have been, and might still be, and it made me feel physically sick. I sat there for over an hour, a thousand thoughts going through my mind. I was angry and confused about what I was feeling. In the end I couldn't fight back the tears any longer. I sat on the sofa and cried more uncontrollably than I ever had before. Jackie must have heard me and came downstairs, shocked by my show of emotion and held me tightly. I'd never cried so much and I felt like screaming the house down with pure frustration just as I had done all those years before.

For the next week my mind turned everything over and over, never finding any answers or any comfort apart from the fact that I could be fairly confident the children were now in a safe place. I couldn't sleep or rest because my thoughts and worries of what might have happened to the children were so loud in my head.

I tried so many times to get their mother to talk to me but she didn't answer my calls and eventually the phone number went dead. She must have been too embarrassed to admit what had been going on and, obviously, the authorities wouldn't give me any information beyond the barest facts. It was as if the children had been swallowed up into a huge silence, leaving us to imagine what had been happening to them, but from talking more to my other sisters I began to get a clearer picture about how badly the kids had been treated and how their only hope of a better life would come from being taken into care.

However hard I tried to focus on what was going on in my life now, I kept finding myself being drawn back into the past and remembering how one of my nephews had clung to me when I'd last visited them. Looking back now I realized he must have been starving for some affection. He was a very quiet boy, always ready to please, and the thought of him brought back so many memories of myself at that age. I remembered how desperate I'd been for so long and wondered if it had been the same for him. Questions kept going round and round in my head; they wouldn't stop. I kept winding myself up with the same, constant questions: Could I have done more to help at that stage? Should I be doing more to rescue them now? What should I be doing to help them now? No matter how many times I asked them, I couldn't find answers to any of the questions.

One thought I could take some comfort from was that they were safe now, or at least I thought so.

14

Nowhere to Hide

With all this weighing down my thoughts, I had to start doing the publicity for the book. If I'd been nervous about it before, I was dreading it now, knowing that I wouldn't be able to talk about the one thing that was now uppermost in my mind, the plight of my sister's children and how ashamed and useless I felt that such things were still happening in the Lewis family today.

Once the *Daily Mail* story had been printed I was free to talk to the other journalists who the publishers had set up for me. To my surprise and relief it wasn't too bad talking to one person at a time. They were always attentive and didn't seem to want to pry too much into my past since I suppose it had all been written about in the book. They seemed to just want to get an idea of what I was like now, so they could set the stories from the book into context. Jackie was also interviewed and she handled it brilliantly. She was calm, thoughtful and very beautiful and I glowed with pride at the way in which she was able to just take it all in her stride. There were moments when I felt my courage was beginning to build. Maybe, I thought to myself, this isn't going to be such a frightening ordeal after all. But then the enormity of what might be about to happen when I saw *The*

Kid in the shops would make me feel mixed emotions, partly excited that people would actually want to read my book and partly nervous because I knew I had not yet dealt with the past.

The book came out on time and I saw stacks of them appearing in the shops as their staff took delivery and set them out. The newspaper interviews began to appear in print and they were very supportive. Everyone seemed to be really laidback about it all and this started to bring a smile back to my face. This once again spurred me on to work harder and in turn suppressed my childhood thoughts. Other journalists I hadn't even met read the book and wrote about it in reviews. There was an article in the *London Evening Standard* in which the journalist called on the newly appointed Minister for Children to read the book and not to 'ignore the harrowing message'.

One of my first radio interviews didn't start as well as expected. Before I went to the studio I was told that a researcher would call to discuss the book. She would then get an idea of the questions to give the DJ for me to answer, which seemed like a good idea. A time was agreed when she would call, so when the phone rang I thought I had prepared myself to answer whatever questions she might have.

'So,' she said, 'tell me about your book.'

No one up to that point had asked me that question and it completely stumped me. How could I explain *The Kid* in a few sentences down the phone if she didn't know anything about me or the story? What was I going to say: 'Ah, yes, I was beaten and tortured by my parents'?

I could never be that forthright, as if I was proud about my past.

I couldn't find the words to answer, so all I could say was, 'It's about my life. Do you have any questions for me?'

She was obviously at as much of a loss of what to ask as I was of what to say and we finished the conversation as quickly as we decently could. Afraid that I had messed up I called my publishers and from what I gathered they didn't seem too impressed with the researcher's approach. Apparently she hadn't even seen the book and they agreed I couldn't have been expected to answer such an open-ended question. I could understand her problem. She couldn't possibly read every book that they talked about on the programme, there wouldn't be enough hours in the day. The interview was put on hold and the lady called back a few days later full of apologies, but I told her I was fine about it and was sorry for not being able to answer her first question. By then she had scanned the parts of the book that they wanted to feature on their programme and she asked me some questions that I was able to reply to. The interview itself took place shortly afterwards with the radio DJ and I answered his questions live on air with no problem.

After that I would go into radio stations, wait to be interviewed and if the presenter had a copy of the book on the desk I would ask them politely if they could please turn it over, or better still put it out of sight. Some were a little surprised by the request, believing I would and should be proud of what I had written. I knew I would feel that way eventually, but only when I had proved that I could move away from my past, to myself, my family and everyone who now knew about me. It was hard work talking out loud about my life to strangers, particularly in the artificial surroundings of a radio studio. Being interviewed reminded me of being asked so many questions over the years by social workers, foster parents, doctors and police and never being able to tell them about the things that happened in that house. When things had got so bad that I had managed to say something I was ignored. But now I thought that if I could finally talk about it then it would be like me walking out of that room once and for all and closing the door behind me.

The good thing was that I had been able to control and lock away the bad childhood habits that had reappeared a few months before by thinking of the future, as I always had done before I started writing about the past. This I thought was a start to handling what was going on inside my head. Whenever the interviewers asked me about the future the tone of my voice changed, my face would light up and I could feel my spirits rising, because there were so many things I wanted to do and talk about, so many plans bubbling away in my head that always made me feel good and helped me forget my past. Each time this happened I became more determined to get a grip of what had happened to me and put it away once and for all.

Everyone involved with the publication of the book was thrilled by all the attention but, although I could see it was good for the book and that it was going well, I felt exposed and vulnerable as the publicity spread. The thing

I found most difficult was making eye contact with strangers and so I started wearing my sunglasses even when it wasn't that sunny, erecting a barrier between me and everyone else and, more importantly, between me and my past. I took to wearing them whenever I was outside the house. It was as if they gave me a kind of protection, making me feel less naked and hiding my vulnerability. They covered me up from the feeling that I had first experienced when walking through the offices of Michael Joseph all those months before. They allowed me to maintain an illusion of privacy from the public and a screen from the full impact of the truths I had revealed to myself. As the book spread and my children could see copies of it clearly on the shelves in the shops, it wasn't long before they started to ask questions. 'What's the book about? Can I read it?' my daughter would ask. I tried to put off answering but children are naturally inquisitive. Eventually all I could say was that 'Daddy's parents weren't very nice to him when he was small.' She looked at me intently and then asked the inevitable question.

'Why?'

I couldn't answer. Instead I promised that they could read the book when they were a little older. That seemed to satisfy them, for now anyhow.

Shortly after the start of the publicity we were told that the *This Morning* TV programme wanted Jackie and me to go on and be interviewed by Fern Britton and Phillip Schofield. Neither of us was sure we were up to it. When talking to newspaper or radio journalists, we were at least invisible to the rest of the world. People might read or hear my words, but they couldn't actually look at my face as I said them, they couldn't see the emotions in my eyes. It was going to be a big jump to talk on live television and we weren't sure how we would react under such pressure. The publishers told me that this was to be the final interview and would be just what the book needed. I knew I couldn't say no and, in fact, the idea of going into a television studio was very appealing. I was eager to see with my own eyes what went on as I was still trying to get into film school.

The publishers had worked so hard on my behalf and this was a big feather in their caps. If this went well sales of the book were likely to take off very fast, although *The Kid* was already creeping up the bestseller charts, having reached about number six in a matter of weeks. We were told about the programme around a week before we were due to go on. Jackie and I had a long chat that evening in the kitchen and decided we should give it a go. We told ourselves we had nothing to lose and everything to gain.

It was doubly hard to make these sorts of decisions when the one thing that was still going round and round in my mind was the plight of the children who had recently been taken away from my sister. I had been trying to find out what had happened to them, but just couldn't get any information. It was as if they had disappeared into a black hole. So much was going on in such a short time that I didn't know how to deal with it and I was afraid of tripping up or, worse still, showing my true emotions on live television.

'We just have to be ourselves,' Jackie and I agreed, once we'd decided to go ahead. So it was all set and we were booked in for the programme.

The morning of the show we were collected early by car and taken to the studios in London. I guess they wanted to be sure we turned up and didn't back out at the last minute. We arrived on time and were led through what seemed like a warehouse on London's South Bank which was filled with costumes and large stage sets, and then through a labyrinth of offices, until eventually we were shown into a dressing room next to Joan Collins.

We were met there by Jess, our publicity representative from Penguin, and were introduced to the people from the *This Morning* programme who were going to be looking after us during our stay. I think Jess was really there to hold our hands in this strange, new world and I must admit her familiar face was a welcome sight. It wasn't long before we were then escorted to make-up.

'Make-up?' I squawked. 'I'm not having make-up!'

Jackie and Jess chuckled to one another, united by their gender, and took no notice of my protests. I followed begrudgingly behind them into the make-up room. I sat down where I was told to in front of a large mirror with light bulbs all around, just like in the movies. I looked in horror at the table in front of me, which was covered in different types of stuff to put on your face. Jackie and Jess laughed at my expression and warned the make-up lady about my concerns. She just smiled and explained that she would only put a little powder on my face to stop 'the shine', giving me visions of my face looking like a prize egg on live television. As she reached into the make-up pile I was relieved when she just picked up one small pot and brush. As she started brushing the powder stuff on my face I just kept dead still with my eyes closed. As soon as she'd finished powdering and I was wiping my eyes and face, to the continuing amusement of Jackie and Jess, we were then taken back to the dressing room and introduced to some people whose names I couldn't remember because my brain was beginning to seize up with nerves at the prospect of stepping in front of the cameras.

Jackie could tell that I was getting more and more agitated as the moment of exposure approached. This interview was going to be going out live to millions of people. It was different to anything I'd ever attempted before. Until a few months earlier I'd never told anyone about my past and now I was going to be telling millions of complete strangers. They would all be able to see me and I wouldn't be able to see any of them. They would be able to see right into my eyes through the cameras. When you're talking to a newspaper journalist you have time to explain what you're trying to say and to make sure that you're making sense. Here I would have just a few minutes and anything stupid I might say by mistake would be broadcast directly into the homes of millions of viewers. I was wondering what kind of questions they would ask and, more to the point, whether I would have the courage to answer them.

Jackie and I fidgeted the time away nervously exchanging jokes as we waited to be fetched for the final few yards of the walk towards the studio and waiting cameras.

A few minutes before we were due to go into the studio we were escorted to the Green Room, where everyone waited for their turn to step into the spotlight. Jess was still with us as we stepped into the busy room, filled with familiar faces coming and going. Everyone seemed to know one another so Jackie and I sat together at one end of the sofa, quietly waiting our turn.

Above all the buzz of the Green Room the words 'Be yourself, be yourself, be yourself,' kept going round and round in my head. I'd put my sunglasses into my pocket, just in case I couldn't take it and began to get upset and had to hide my eyes at the last minute.

Then a man whose face looked vaguely familiar from the television came in and sat beside me.

'So, what are you on for?' he asked cheerfully, attempting to strike up a conversation.

Again it was the worst question I could have been asked at that moment. I opened my mouth, but no words came out and again I didn't know what to say.

'Kevin's talking about his book,' Jess interjected, seeing that I needed some help.

'What's it about?' he asked.

Just in time a voice interrupted us and we were called to go through to the studio. Jackie went first, I followed and Jess waited in the Green Room for us to return. The heavy doors to the studio opened to let us in. It was dead quiet inside, with Fern and Phillip doing the interview before us. The first thing I noticed was the immense heat that the lights were creating. To the right of me was a black booth with row upon row of monitors all showing different angles from different camera shots. Watching them intently were a line of people who seemed to be whispering directions to the people on the studio floor. I was taken aback by the intense, subdued buzz and heat of the place.

It was at that moment that I finally realized the importance of what I had written and the impact the book would have on the lives contained inside it. I could see just what a big deal this was, something even more out of my experience than I had been imagining. I was feeling desperately out of my depth.

We were escorted across to a set of sofas where we were to wait for Fern and Phillip to come over to sit with us after finishing whatever it was they were doing before our item. I sat as close to Jackie as I could get, every muscle in my body tight with nerves. I could feel tears welling up behind my eyes already, my throat tightening and making swallowing difficult. I could tell Jackie was nervous too, but as always she was completely in control and put her hand on mine to try to steady me down, like you might with a horse before a big race. While I was waiting on the sofa I lifted my head and I could see people all over the studio looking at me. I felt sure they all knew who I was and everything about my life, while I knew nothing about any of them. I tried not to make eye contact with anyone. Even breathing was proving to be a struggle.

Then I realized it was happening. The cameras and lights were shining in our direction. Fern and Phillip were talking about us and at that moment we were visible to all those watching. Fern was walking over to sit on a chair next to me as she talked and Phillip was behind her. The cameras were on us and everything seemed to be closing in.

Both Phillip and Fern greeted us warmly and then Fern began asking questions. I started to talk but I could feel my voice becoming choked as I struggled to answer, desperate to keep my composure. Everything came into sharp focus in my head, right there on that sofa, about what I'd written and what was happening today. I tried to reach into my pocket and get my sunglasses out, but I couldn't get my hand to move. I could feel myself becoming more and more upset as I fought to keep control of my voice and suppress my tears.

I wanted to talk about my sister's children who'd just been taken into care, to say that the things that had happened to me were still happening to other children and that we had to do something to help, but I couldn't do that here. It wasn't the place to say what I wanted to say. I didn't know enough about what had happened and I was ashamed to think that such a thing was still happening in the Lewis family. I had to force my mind back to talking selfishly about myself and what happened to me all those years ago.

When I looked across at Fern I could see tears welling up in her eyes, just as they had in the eyes of the publishers when I first met them. That was still the last thing I wanted. I didn't want people to feel sorry for me or to get upset about my past. I wanted to show them that I was happy today.

'Are you all right?' I asked Fern. 'Would you like a tissue?'

I wanted to get Fern a tissue, but then someone

appeared out of shot to hand her one and she dabbed at her eyes as Phillip took over the questioning to give her time to recover. Seeing Fern get upset made me more uneasy. I really needed my sunglasses now, but again I couldn't get my hand into my pocket to get them out. I wanted to escape from all the eyes that were looking at me around the studio, from the glare of the lights and from the cameras, which seemed to be closing in. I wanted to crawl back and hide inside myself, covering my face like I did as a child when I was upset. I didn't want to be seen on television crying, as if I couldn't cope. I kept on trying to get the glasses out at the same time as answering another question, but I couldn't get at them and I felt naked and exposed as I had so many times since putting my life down on paper. I felt a tear roll down my cheek.

Suddenly it was all over and they went to a commercial break. The hustle of the studio staff took over as they prepared for the moment when they went back on air. I stood up straight away, immediately putting my hand into my pocket. The glasses slid easily out, I quickly put them over my eyes as the tears started, thankful for the relief of cutting out the glare and giving me a little privacy. I could feel everyone in the room staring at me, but now they couldn't see my eyes any more.

'Are you OK?' Fern asked, as the glasses covered my eyes. 'Have you got a headache? The lights are very powerful in here.'

'I want to go home,' I said in a quiet voice, my bottom lip trembling.

Fern and I gave each other a hug. I shook Phillip's

hand and headed out of the studio unescorted with my head down, leaving Jackie behind to find her own way back to the dressing room. I was met outside and taken back to the dressing room where Jess was waiting for us. Jackie came in shortly afterwards. I'd shot out of the studio so quickly that I still had the microphone clipped on to me. It was removed in the dressing room while I tried to compose myself behind my glasses. I kept them on as we made small talk. I think they all knew how desperately I wanted to go home and so the car was quickly brought round. When I came out of the dressing room I walked past the make-up artist I'd been talking to earlier and she put her arms around me. I said nothing.

They asked if there was anything else we wanted to do while we had the car and driver at our disposal. We just wanted to go. We needed the security of home.

I kept the glasses on all the way home, barely talking, staring out of the window, trying to make sense of what I'd done and what had happened. After a while a smile crept back on to my face as I thought of the first time I had to wear make-up. I began to chuckle. Jackie asked what I was laughing at and I told her. We both started laughing and smiling for the rest of the journey home. It was as if the dark clouds that had been following me were finally lifting.

Later that afternoon the publicity people from Michael Joseph told us they had heard that during the *This Morning* interview everyone in the studio had stopped whatever they were doing to listen and watch the monitors. We were told that the place was completely silent, people's eyes fixed on the screens.

Well, whatever emotions the pressure had unleashed in me must have come across on the screen because the public reacted unbelievably to the interview and the book started to sell beyond even the publisher's wildest expectations. I didn't have to worry about promoting it any more because now people were telling one another about it, recommending it to friends. Reviews were appearing and we shot on up the bestseller charts, even passing Hillary Clinton who had just published her autobiography, arriving at number two beneath Bill Bryson's latest work. The publishers kept telling me it was a fairy tale, that such things only happened occasionally.

Finally my brother Wayne called and said that he had read the book and had rung to wish me luck. He told me he didn't have any arguments with anything I'd written.

'There was one factual mistake,' he said.

'What was that?' I asked.

'You said we went to the hospital after Dennis threw the knife at me, but it was the doctor's surgery. You were too young to have known the difference. Everything else is just as I remember.'

He'd even read parts of it to Gloria.

'What did she say?' I asked.

'She just denied it.'

I didn't care.

15

Given the Chance at Last

By the time summer arrived I was ready to put everything behind me and was eager to move forward in my newly chosen career. In preparation I had read and deconstructed over thirty movie scripts. I had studied their layouts, how they explained their angles, camera shots, internal and external, and every other detail of the film. I tried to compare them to what I had done myself and to what I had in mind with my childhood scribbles on the walls. What amazed me was how the written word could be turned into film, brought to life in each scene, how each shot was explained with such clarity that you could visualize it immediately. Everything I was learning about the medium excited me and drove me on to learn more. It felt as though I was making good use of the past and turning it to my advantage. I had completed my synopses for both my first film script and my first novel. I'd built them up slowly, as I promised myself I would, writing them, then breaking them down again, re-writing over and over until I saw the film and novel with the visual clarity that I'd learnt from the scripts I'd read and studied. But I still needed to learn more about the professions of screenwriting and directing if I wanted to move on to the next stage.

I knew in my heart that this was what I truly wanted to do; the question was how to go about it.

I had already approached virtually every film school I could find, mainly in Britain, and with no luck. I'd even tried some in the US, but the answer was always the same: with little or no formal education, and no experience in the industry, I was not the calibre of pupil they were looking for. The rejections were frustrating, but they didn't discourage me. Every time it happened I would look back at myself silently playing in that squalid room with my dreams all around me. I know I don't have what you would call a formal education, but there can be advantages to that. I was brought up with no parental boundaries to my thinking and my actions, and so I've made my own. I know it's that that drives me forward. I don't question whether I can or cannot do things, I try them anyway, believing that anything is possible. That is probably the only good thing to come out of my past and I intend to cling on to it. Because my parents never taught me where the usual boundaries are, I am often unable to see why other people believe there are things they can't achieve in life.

Anyone who knew anything about the publishing industry, for instance, would have known that it was almost impossible for someone with little education to get their autobiography published when they were still in their early thirties. But I didn't know that, so I did it anyway. Anyone who knew anything about polo would believe that it would be virtually impossible for a grown man with no contacts in that world to take it up if he has only ever ridden a horse once. But

I didn't know that, so I went ahead and did it anyway.

It was the same when I went into the bar business as a young man, and set up a telecommunications company. My attitude to what is possible also helps me with my inventions, leaving me free of doubt and confident that I will be able to bring things together if I just try. Everything I have ever wanted has started as a dream, which I had to make come true. The only way I've ever known how to do that is by breaking the dream down into manageable pieces or goals, then tackling them one by one. As each section was completed I knew I was getting close to the end result. So I wasn't about to give up on this one, the one I considered the most important in my career and the one that would help me make constructive use of my past. It was a career I had chosen and was determined to achieve.

I have to admit that for a little while I did consider the possibility of lying about my education just to get a break, but decided against it. I'd gone a lot further in my life than most people my age. I believed completely that I had it in me to move on and achieve whatever else I wanted to achieve. So I kept on searching on the computer and one summer evening I came up with a new name, the Raindance film school. I've tried everyone else, I thought, no harm in trying one more. I sent for their details and a few days later an envelope arrived. I opened it and numerous leaflets slid out on to the kitchen table. There were courses for everything that anyone who wanted to get into the film industry might need; directing, producing, cinematography, 35mm, 16mm, digital sound, lighting, scriptwriting, everything from low-budget movie making to Hollywood blockbusters. It looked very impressive and a tingle of excitement ran through me as I read on.

As I scanned the brochures I could see that they didn't specify anywhere what qualifications or previous experience were needed in order to subscribe to the courses. I was used to phoning and trying to convince those on the other end of the line to take me, so I dialled their number and told the woman who answered what I wanted to do. She explained when the courses started, what they cost and so on. It got to the end of the call and I was going to have to make my usual admission.

'I don't have any educational qualifications or experience,' I confessed, expecting that to be the end of the call as usual.

'If you have the drive, the ambition, and believe you have the ability to write and direct,' she replied, 'then that's fine.'

She had blown the problem away as if it wasn't of any interest to her, saying exactly the words I had been wanting to hear, the ones that I believed with my whole heart were true. I was taken aback, my heart thudding, and said I'd call again soon. I put the phone down and went back through the course literature to work out exactly what I wanted to do, unable to believe my luck. I scooped up all the brochures, which by then had fallen on the floor, and went through them one by one, grinning insanely. I called Jackie, who was out shopping.

'I've found a place that will take me!' I shouted gleefully.

'That's brilliant,' she said. 'When do you start?'

'Haven't booked it yet, call you back,' I said, breathless with excitement.

I was eager to make my choices and ring the film school before they changed their minds. When I got them back on the line we had another long conversation, by the end of which I had booked several different courses to give myself a rounded view of the film industry, with the main emphasis on directing, producing and writing. I put the phone down at the end and punched the air with an excited clench of the fists and a big 'Yes'. It was going to be six months of hard, intensive courses and I was so looking forward to it I could hardly wait. It would start after the summer. Everything was starting to fit into place perfectly.

I was so proud of myself for having kept trying and for not giving up at the first discouragement. Through perseverance I had found somewhere that would take me for who I was, not for what certificates I had. The school had always been there; it hadn't changed its policy just for me, but because I'd searched and searched I had found it. I could have given up the search back in January, when all the rejections were making me ask myself whether I was just dreaming, and whether they were all right and I was wrong. But because of my own ambition and determination I had managed to get a foot on the ladder. I knew there was still a long way to go and I was under no illusion that the really hard work would begin after film school had finished, when I was out in the market, trying to sell my film and to prove what I could do. My eyes were wide open, wider than they had ever been before and I knew problems and difficulties lay ahead, but I was feeling great about the future challenges. In a way it helped me to smooth over my past once more, as if I had turned the clock back two years to a time before I had even thought about tackling my past. Gloria and Dennis were slowly fading away.

I knew for sure now what I wanted to do with my life and how I was going to go about it. I was determined to continue to move slowly, gradually building the blocks of my career. Having got through the launch of the book and having started putting my past firmly behind me, I felt great. I was beginning to hold my head up high with my smile returning once more.

16

Summer Had Finally Arrived

The book had acquired a life of its own now, gaining momentum and going up the charts. Little was required of me by the publishers beyond the odd phone call. My time was my own, for me to do whatever I wanted with. Rarely does someone get a whole free summer, but I did and I was determined to make the most of it.

When I wasn't with Jackie and the kids, I spent most of my spare time on the polo fields at Knepp Castle. I loved the wide-open spaces of the fields stretching out beneath the castle, and the buzz there would be before the game started, with the ponies groomed like princes and princesses neatly lined up at the side of their horseboxes. I must admit it felt a little strange, me and my pony Mistico up against the other players with their string of ponies.

By the time the book promotion work was more or less completed the polo season was well under way and I was itching to join in and play. I had been a little apprehensive about joining a polo club, having heard so many things about it being a snobby game and only for the upper classes and the rich and the famous. So before joining the club Jackie and I were invited to dinner one evening with a few of its members to make sure I wouldn't feel too out of place. It was a great evening and now I'd met some of the people I felt a lot more comfortable about joining. I had bought my boots, knee-pads, white jeans and polo stick and Mistico was to be stabled at Knepp. I was ready to go and eager to get out on to the field.

I could also see the funny side of the boy from New Addington playing the sport of maharajas and princes. The first time I put on my outfit I burst out laughing as I looked at myself in the mirror. I looked like someone auditioning for the Village People. It made me realize how far I had moved away from my past, and I saw it as yet another reason why I should forget about my childhood. I imagined turning up at King Henry's Drive or anywhere during my previous life dressed in white jeans and knee-high boots! I couldn't stop laughing.

Because I was a beginner I was at first put into teams to make up the numbers. If someone needed a minus-two player then I would be able to enter. That was fine by me. I just wanted to play and I needed all the practice and experience I could get.

As well as practising my game, I had to learn basic skills: how to saddle up Mistico, how to groom him and look after the tack. My groom that season was Stacey who helped me with everything. But even at the end of the season I still hadn't got the hang of tacking up Mistico. I was always too excited and eager to get out and play. Luckily Stacey was on hand to help and I was happy to leave it to her. I would arrive early and usually stay to the last game, keen to watch the professionals playing. It was an awesome sight and gave me the same tingle that I had that day when I first stumbled on to the sport. Watching these skilled players on their ponies charging around the field with such control, it seemed effortless, and a great way for me to learn. I would sit studying how they sat into their saddles while taking their shots, how they went from full gallop to a standstill, turning their ponies on the spot and repositioning themselves for the next play. There was so much to learn from just observing, but it was practising and playing that seemed to me to be the best way to improve.

In time I found that I had a good eye for the ball, the problem was I needed to get my pony into the right place at the right moment without falling off. Because I didn't always position Mistico correctly I would often have to lean much further out to reach the ball than gravity could stand and I spent large parts of my early games on the ground looking at his backside. Mistico was getting so used to me falling off that he would stand there, waiting patiently for me to clamber back on. I was pretty sure I could see him laughing at me as he looked down at my prone body on the ground every few minutes. My language was not improving that summer either.

I tried to concentrate on staying in my position on the field, even though I wasn't the best rider in the world. The good riders had such control of their ponies while I was still feeling nervous if mine started to get a bit jumpy. Although I was getting much more confident around him, that confidence was easily unseated! If I took him out a bucket of feed and he cantered up to me I would be hopping behind a fence to get out of the way.

I knew I had to overcome this and spent as much time as I could with him, touching him, grooming him, getting comfortable around him. It was so soothing and comfortable as we both got to know one another a little bit more. Sometimes I would just stand there with Mistico by my side and we both seemed equally contented. In those precious moments I would forget all about my past.

Like most people I had preconceived ideas about the polo world before I experienced it for myself, but all I saw during that summer was people from every walk of life coming together for a sport that they were passionate about. There was none of the snobbery that I had first imagined there would be and the social scene was not compulsory – it was there if you wanted it and if you didn't, then so be it. At first I kept myself to myself, just practising and watching, but so many people in the club were so enthusiastic about the sport that you couldn't help but be affected by their love for the game. The professional players could see that I was trying hard to improve and would come up to me and give me advice about how to improve my play. It was a lovely feeling, and something that I was always in awe of because these people did it for no other reason than to help my game so that I would enjoy it more.

I knew that if I really wanted to improve then I had to ride better. I had initially dismissed it as a mere detail but it was now obvious it was the most important skill I needed to acquire. So I began having lessons with Claire, a player who lived not far from me and also played at Knepp. Each morning I would arrive for lessons using her ponies, which I was grateful for, and slowly but surely, with lots of trial and error and determination, my riding began to improve. I was able to position myself correctly and consequently spent less time on the floor and more time in the saddle, which was a great relief to my fellow team players, to Mistico and to my backside. As I improved I began being selected more to play in games because I could always hit the ball and looked out for my position on the field. Consequently I was giving fewer fouls and less advantage to opposing teams. I teamed up with one of the club professionals by the name of Martin and played with him for the rest of the summer. For the last few games I entered my own team. At first I didn't know what to call my team: Kid? No. Kev's Polo Team? Definitely not! Then I came up with Mojo. Mojo Polo Team, I thought, that'll work. The fact that I'd recently been studying the script for *Austin Powers* might have had something to do with it. I looked up the meaning of the word, which is 'magic charm' or 'spell'. It sounded just right – a magical spell to get rid of my past – and so it stuck for the rest of the season.

Even though I didn't win anything that season, I still had a great time in my somewhat limited capacity. I'd made many new friends and towards the end of the season I met up with Martin again. He convinced me that the best way to improve both my riding and play would be to go to Argentina, the home of polo. Jackie knew how passionate I was about the sport and thought it would do me the world of good. I agreed to join him for ten days in Argentina in January. The best thing of all was that now on the odd occasion when Gloria would return to my thoughts I would take a deep breath and imagine the smell of the freshly cut grass and the sight of Mistico playing in the field, happy with his new home, and it seemed that I could just blow the memories of Gloria away.

17
Other People's Stories

A few weeks after the book had been released and people had had a chance to read it, I started to receive letters, forwarded on in batches from the publishers. When I received the first batch I was, to say the least, surprised. In my heart I had known that I wasn't the only person ever to have suffered a bad childhood, and that had been confirmed for me by what was happening to my sister's children, but now I was hearing stories from all over the country which showed that my experience, tragically, was far from unique. The fact that I had been able to find a way to make my voice heard meant that some of the others too were now able to sit down and write letters detailing what had happened to them or to people they knew or loved.

Some of the letters were from people who had been in similar situations to mine and were asking for help or advice on how to deal with the scars and the memories. To begin with I didn't know what to say to them. How could I have answered their letters when I was only just about getting to grips with what I had written? So all I could do was wish them luck for the future. The best letters to receive though were the ones where the writers told me that the book had given them the courage to go out and do something with their own lives after having suffered a bad start. It made me feel good. If I had made just one person realize it was possible to escape from a bad past then the whole project had been worthwhile.

One or two of them were looking back to their own childhoods, in much the same way as I'd done in the book, and I would try to encourage them to look forward instead, like I had with Robert. There was nothing they could do to change what had happened in the past, but they could make their futures into anything they wanted.

I made sure I replied to absolutely everyone who had given me a return address. I felt that if they'd gone to the trouble of writing to me the least I could do was write back. I replied to their questions as best I could, telling them what I do, and suggesting that they should make a plan for the future, breaking it down bit by bit so that they could actually see how to get to their final goal, but not forgetting that it's OK to change your goal as you move up the ladder. I felt that writing back to them was a constructive thing to do, but also as I kept writing it down it felt as if I was reinforcing my own resolve.

Some letters were disturbing. A number of people wrote to say they knew of children who were having things done to them that were similar to what I'd been through and wondered what they should do. Some of them were neighbours of abused kids, or the parents of their friends; others were relations who didn't know whether they should interfere or not as they were concerned this would bring more trouble to the children from their persecutors. Some wrote of how they weren't able to cope with their past and had tried to take their own lives. Others wrote to say that their brother or sister had ended their lives. There were also letters from parents who believed they had given their children everything, only to see them going off the rails. Some wanted to know why abused children so often cover up for their parents. I knew the answer to that: it was simply fear. Fear of the parents and what they might do if they found out. Fear of what would happen if no one came to help and fear of where they might end up if they were taken away, and also fear of what their friends would think. An abused child nearly always knows they want to get out, but can't see what needs to be done.

The problems of a bad start seemed to travel with many people into their adult lives, a fact which I hadn't accepted until recently.

A grandmother wrote to me about her six-year-old granddaughter and three-year-old grandson. Her daughter was a heroin addict and the children had been taken into care, but now they had been sent back to the derelict house where their mother lived and her granddaughter was having to look after her grandson. The grandmother was afraid to intervene or tell Social Services because every time any officials went round they made matters worse, leaving the children in an even more vulnerable and frightening position. What made it worse was that it was such a horribly familiar story.

Another letter arrived from a mother who knew of a

girl who was going through much the same as I went through. She was a friend of her daughter. She told me the child was sleeping on a mattress on the floor with no lightbulb in her room. Her mother hated her just as Gloria hated me. The woman had found out about this when the child was ill and her mother threw her out of the house, not wanting her under her feet all day. The woman had given the girl all the support she could, including hot meals daily, love and encouragement. The girl had told her that she had believed she lived a normal life until she was shown otherwise. The girl didn't want Social Services involved because of her brothers and sisters, who the mother seemed to like. She was planning to leave home at sixteen, which was not far away. The writer said that the child's mother was a loud, overbearing and intimidating woman.

She went on to say that she felt guilty, ashamed and embarrassed for not being able to do more for fear of what would happen to the child behind closed doors. She then asked for my advice. I told her to speak to the NSPCC or Childline and to get the girl to ask their advice, but to continue to support her whenever she could. I assured her that the girl would always remember her acts of kindness and it would at least show her that the world was not always a cruel place to live in. As I read the letter I admired this girl's courage and that of her friend's mother.

I thought about what this woman was saying and it seemed to me she had hit on the biggest problem for children who are being abused by their parents or guardians; everyone is frightened to say anything for fear of retaliation and of making things worse for the children involved. And so we hesitate too long before doing anything. It's the same problem that teachers have with children who are being bullied at school. They can tell the bullies off or punish them, but they can't be with the children every hour of the day, so eventually the bullies are going to get access to their victims again and they are going to be even keener to hurt them as revenge for what they would see as a betrayal. When anyone goes to the rescue of a child in trouble, they have to be able to take them away from the instigator of the trouble there and then if they want to be effective. They can't hope that just by issuing a warning they're going to make anything better. But for that to happen the child in trouble needs to find the courage to speak out, so the situation becomes a stalemate and the most vulnerable people in society, the abused children, are trapped beyond the reach of those who could be in a position to help.

I remember so vividly the social worker asking me, in front of my parents, whether I wanted to stay with them or be taken into care – there was no way I could have found the courage to speak the truth at that moment, and I was anxious to hide my past away, being frightened of the possible repercussions of speaking out. At the same time the authorities can't go round taking children away from their parents every time they hear a rumour about maltreatment. There are certain procedures that have to be gone through, during which the children nearly always have to stay where they are, with their abusers. One thing that was clearly apparent was how long it took for the authorities to intervene on behalf of these vulnerable children. I don't know if we will ever be able to find a solution to this tragic catch-22.

The letters made me cry with frustration. I'd heard so many social workers and politicians saying that the sort of experiences I'd had as a child couldn't happen any more, but it was becoming increasingly obvious to me that there would always be children who would slip through the net of the welfare system and who would be left in the care of inadequate and violent parents or guardians for at least part of their childhood, if not all of it. This fact was being brought home even more force-fully by the problems that my sister's children were having, and it was about to be hammered home harder than I could ever have imagined.

18

Disbelief and Frustration

The last I'd heard about my sister's children was that they had been taken into temporary foster care until their ultimate fate could be decided. I was assured they were all together with a family. Whatever they had been put through in the past, they had reached a safe haven now, or so I believed. I still hadn't spoken to their mother, my sister, who was obviously too ashamed to talk to me, but then I received a call from another sister, the one who had broken the news to me to begin with.

She told me that an official working on behalf of the children in care was asking if there was anyone in the Lewis family who could take on any of the children. She had asked both my sisters and, to my amazement, my sister told me that they were both considering the possibility.

I was horrified. Both of them were struggling with bringing up five and six children each as it was. One had a partner, the other didn't. Money was tight, to say the least. The idea of giving them more children to look after was ridiculous, but they were actually thinking of agreeing, truly believing that it would be better for the kids than having them stay in care, as if being with blood relatives was always better, no matter what the circumstances. I knew that they were doing it out of guilt but that was the wrong motive, especially with the pressures of their already strained and difficult lives.

I pleaded with her to see sense and to realize that the children would be far better off in care, being looked after by people who had the necessary experience and resources, even if they weren't their real family. What astonished me more than anything was that the authorities would even consider burdening a single mum, who had virtually no money or resources, with eight children in total.

Most stunning of all, however, was the news that Gloria had volunteered to take some of the children herself, no doubt seeing them as a potential source of income from the State. You would think such a suggestion would have been dismissed out of hand, but the authorities were actually considering the possibility.

I was appalled. The very idea of it sent a shiver of fear down my spine. It was even worse than what had happened to me. Although they had sent me back to Gloria from the children's home where I was so happy, at least I had had a few years' respite in which to gather my self-esteem and self-confidence before being forced back into the mayhem, but these kids would hardly have had time to unpack before they found themselves shunted back into an abusive household and into the power of a woman who was already known to act violently towards them.

How could such a thing happen? The idea of another generation of innocent children being handed over to someone who was completely unable to stop herself from beating and bullying anyone weaker than herself left me feeling there was no hope of ever improving the situation for any abused children. I found it hard to understand how there could be a bestselling book in all the shops that detailed some of the things Gloria had done to her own children, but the authorities were still able to consider her as a potential guardian for her grandchildren. Pictures of what she'd done to me and my nephews and nieces and what she would be able to do to them in the future if she got hold of them stirred vividly in my mind.

The lady who had been instructed to make the enquiries into the situation also asked my sister to ask me whether Jackie and I would be willing to take any of the children on ourselves. The idea of coping with the pressure of taking on another child from the Lewis family terrified me. I felt awful to have to say no, but I was only just starting to get on top of my own life and there was no way I could face the prospect of jeopardizing my kids' happiness by volunteering for a task I was almost certainly not emotionally capable of handling yet. I was in a state of complete disbelief about the whole situation. It seemed as though the authorities knew nothing of the past, because if they did then why were they considering Gloria after all she had done? That, out of everything, was the most frightening concept. I was absolutely lost for words. Although I was no longer angry about what had happened to me in my past, I was now growing furious about the way in which these children were being dealt with today.

Even if I couldn't give them a home myself, however,

I could certainly do something to try to protect them today. I got the number of the woman who was making these enquiries and rang her a few days later, after I had had time to gather my thoughts and calm down. I introduced myself and then kept quiet. I didn't want to say much at first, wanting to hear what she had to say before going on the attack. In my mind I must have been expecting to come up against the same kind of social workers I had as a child, or some bureaucratic monster who would refuse to see why I was making so much of a fuss, but I listened anyway, in order to be sure that my sister had understood the situation correctly.

The lady, whose name was Carol, told me that the children were safe and seemed to be happy now. She was assigned as their legal guardian until their future was decided. Her job was to report back to the courts as to what would be best for the children in the future. She then went on to explain that the children had their own psychologists and independent advisers, including her, who were only interested in what was best for them. As she talked more I realized that she was speaking from her heart, and that she really did have the children's best interests in mind. But then I asked about Gloria and she assured me that it was true Gloria had asked to have some of the children, but that her request had been rejected because she only had a one-bedroom flat. I was so relieved to hear that she wasn't being considered, but I was also amazed that they only dismissed her because her flat was too small, not because she was known to be violent towards children.

I asked Carol if she knew anything about the Lewis

family and she admitted to having seen the article in the *Mail*. We spoke for what seemed like ages and I discovered that despite everything that had happened in the past, no one in authority seemed to have any historical information on the Lewis family on file, even though there had been pages of reports written on the children in question while the Social Services pondered whether or not they should intervene.

How could it be that Gloria could be considered for even a second to be a suitable guardian just because she was related to them? How could it be that there was no file on her anywhere?

As we spoke further Carol explained that it was standard procedure to try to find someone in the family who might be suitable to take the children, but in the circumstances of the Lewis family I didn't think it was right. I thought it would put extra pressure on the natural parent to see someone else in the family bringing up their children, especially with as much history as the Lewis family, and this would also put pressure on the children to regularly see their natural parent while not living with them. The calm way in which Carol explained it all to me made me understand why they had to try, but I was adamant that the children should be able to stay where they were, for the time being anyhow, until somewhere permanent and safe was found for them. The children had escaped from the dreadful estate where they lived within damp, filthy walls and played amongst discarded needles, threatened all the time by drunks and violence. They had been taken somewhere safe and they had to be allowed to stay there. Carol then went on to explain that it was her job to report on the way Social Services had handled this case and admitted she was dismayed at how long it had taken for these children to be taken into care when there was clear evidence of abuse. It was towards the end of the conversation that I had to admit to something that I was ashamed to say.

'None of these children should go back to anyone in the Lewis family if they are to have a chance in life,' I said, hating the fact that I had to say something so terrible about my own family. 'Send them my love.'

She agreed and told me she was going to advise that the younger children be sent for adoption and the older ones should be put forward for long-term fostering. At the end of the conversation I gave her my number and said that if she needed anything else then to please give me a call. As I put the phone down I felt relieved that she genuinely had the children's best interests at heart. I just hoped that there were more people like this woman working in the system.

As I calmed down from the idea of Gloria having the children, I began to think again about the question Carol had asked as to whether Jackie and I would consider taking on one of the children. It played on my mind long after I had put the phone down. I couldn't get the picture of my nephew and the way he had clung to me when I visited out of my mind. Jackie and I talked it over that evening, but we could see no way round it. Our life was coming together, our children were happy and settled and if we did take on this child the last thing we could bear was Gloria and my sister turning up at the house, insisting on seeing him. He was a lovely boy and what made it harder was that he reminded me so much of myself, but I also knew that when I was taken into care the one thing I hated the most was going back to visit my mother and father. I missed my brothers and sisters but, after what they had done, Gloria and Dennis were the last people I wanted to see. I would have dreaded being taken to live with any family member if it might have meant Gloria would still be able to get to me.

I was amazed by how the experiences of my little nephew mirrored my own, with no one taking the blame for what was happening to him and to his brothers and sister, but at least there was some comfort and hope for them now that I had been assured they would not be going to Gloria. I know every situation is different and that some children might want to see their parents after being taken away even if they were their abusers, but unfortunately I can only judge from my own experiences of how I felt in a similar situation. In the end we decided that we couldn't take on any of them because of our own children, who will always come first in our consideration. We also knew that it would bring back to the surface too many damaging emotions and that would be unfair to everyone involved, especially these vulnerable children. We decided that if we took any of them on it would be out of guilt and that would not be the right thing for any child.

Once again I tried to put it all behind me, safe in the knowledge that they were protected. The summer was now over. The polo season had finished and Mistico was resting on a friend's farm over the winter. He was with Claire, the young lady who lived nearby and who had helped me to ride, and I knew I could visit him whenever I needed to. It was now time for me to start film school. After all that had gone on over the previous two years I was looking forward to finally turning my past to good use. It would turn out to be a very productive and enjoyable winter.

19

Film School

The research I'd done into the film industry so far had made me realize that if I wanted to make my dream of becoming a scriptwriter and film director come true I would need to learn a lot and apply myself to my studies with an open mind. Just as I'd had to find someone to help me when I started writing the book, and someone to teach me how to play polo, I needed to find someone who could help me understand how to make movies.

All through the summer I had continued studying scripts and the film business in general, so that I would be as prepared as I could possibly be when it was time to start the course. I remembered clearly that in my childhood, when I was trapped in that dark and dirty room, I would scribble my dreams and could let my imagination go free, scribbling my escape routes on the walls. Now I was planning on making use of the past in a positive way.

I wasn't rushing into it with my eyes shut trying to just get on, as I might have done in the past. My eyes were wide open and I was under no illusion just how hard it would be to break into the industry. I had to start somewhere and Raindance film school seemed to be the best place.

By this time I had eleven different ideas and treatments for films, working them out scene by scene in my large black book that I took with me everywhere I went. But I was horribly aware that nine of them were rubbish. That left me with two that I believed in whole-heartedly. I loved putting them together and I knew I ultimately wanted to create big commercial Hollywood films. I found the easiest way to write the scripts was to picture specific stars in the various roles and then build the characters and dialogue around them. Both my stories were full of action, with the sort of heroes I'd loved as a child, great car chases and finales where good triumphs over evil. I just needed to learn the proper language of how to turn the scenes that I'd mapped out in my head and outlined in a synopsis into real words on the page, so that they could be seen clearly on the screen, just as I had read in the scripts I had studied.

It was an early Saturday morning when I set off to London on the first day of the course. I felt just as I had all those years before when I started a new school, nervous and apprehensive of what lay ahead. I put on my rucksack, which I had filled with notepads, pens, pencils, even a pencil sharpener. All that was missing was a lunch box and crayons! With my bag on my back I set off for my new school. I took the train to Victoria and walked in the fresh morning air across the city to Euston, where I was to enrol on the course. When I arrived the first thing I noticed was that the other students were a wide mixture of ages and types. They weren't all budding young film directors straight out of university as I had first imagined. They came from all walks of life and were carrying similar ambitions as me. My first class was about to start as I arrived and so I settled into a seat in the corner of the classroom, notebook in hand, feeling invigorated by the walk and eager to learn.

Throughout the day I kept myself to myself, unsure how to interact with everyone else to start with, not wanting to get too deep into any conversation in case people started asking me questions about myself, just taking in everything that went on around me. I asked plenty of questions of the teachers, determined to make the most of their knowledge. I didn't tell anyone about my scripts or my plans. I was sure they had plenty of plans of their own and they didn't need to know about mine. I just kept my head down and listened to everything the teachers said. The more I learned over the coming months the more certain I was that movie-making was the industry for me.

As the months went on I found I became comfortable about my abilities and the teaching gave me the confidence to put my scripts into my own style, rather than worrying whether they fitted someone else's criteria, and so in the evenings, once I got back home, I would shut myself away until late, writing my first film script, thinking about how I would write and finding my own style.

As well as having the stories on paper and the pictures in my head of how I wanted those stories to come out on the screen, I was also beginning to realize that my background in the business world would be as valuable to me in filmmaking as any other creative skill. I could see that the people who backed directors needed to be convinced that the directors knew how to use the money they were given effectively, and be sure that they didn't see a budget as something that could just be increased if it proved impossible to manage on what had been allotted. I knew from my experience that if there is a limited amount of money available for a project, then that is what you have to work with.

I believed I could see the secret that lay at the heart of the film business and that differentiated the really successful directors from the rest, allowing them to keep on going in an incredibly cut-throat and competitive industry. They possessed an ability, in simple terms, to put bums on seats, attracting people to go to the cinema and then to buy the resulting DVDs. The key to their success was the quality of the scripts and the actors who played the major roles. It was these two factors that I believed attracted people to the cinemas. One wasn't good enough on its own – a good script could be badly acted and therefore wasted, or a good actor could be wasted on a poor script. But there was one final element that I hadn't thought about, but which was crucial to a film's success, and that was marketing. Getting out to the public and letting them know that your film is coming is vital if you want to get people in front of the screen. If you had an 'A'-list celebrity, a good script, and you marketed it successfully, then the result could be spectacular. So I began to look at these three factors in relation to my own ideas.

While writing I thought about the actors and actresses I wanted to play in the film, growing the characters around them. I could choose who I wanted to use, the best people working in the movies today. I didn't need to care about whether they would actually star in it or not, or whether the budget would support them, because there was nothing to stop me writing with them in mind. It helped a great deal, allowing me once again to work without boundaries. If I didn't think enough of my movies to picture them with a big star in, why would anyone else? And so I let my imagination run wild and it was a great feeling.

I would be writing late into the night, typing through certain scenes faster and faster, my heart racing at the same pace as the action. I could clearly visualize what I was writing and even hear the music that would be in the background as the action unravelled. It was like having a private cinema in my head, just like I'd had as a child when trying to escape from the real world around me. I became as consumed in my fantasy world as I had done when I was in that house. The scenes would give me goosebumps as they unfolded in front of me and I would write for so long that sometimes I was forced to stop because my right hand had swollen painfully from all the typing I was doing. My knuckles have never really recovered from the bare-knuckle fighting I did as a young man, when the skin had become so badly split. I would just have to rest it for a day or so, soaking my hand in warm water, movement slowly returning to my fingers, frustrated at my inability to get back to work again and by the thought that it was scars from my previous life that were holding me back.

I learned so much during that winter. I'm always glad to learn and develop skills, but this was different. I really believed that I was making the best possible use of the past. Whereas I had recently been embarrassed by the revelations in *The Kid*, I now felt I could finally prove that I was not going to let the past get the better of me. What made me even happier was that I had the full support of my family and that I was going to show them and everyone else that it was possible to reach the top through sheer hard work and determination, that you didn't have to let a bad start in life hold you back. In fact I saw it as an advantage.

When it came to the end of the course we had to film a sequence that we would direct, which was based on the television series, *The Bill*, in order to experience the sort of pressures we would have to cope with in the real world. I watched a couple of the other people on the course first and I could see that they were spending too much time talking to the actors who'd been hired for the day and generally fussing about. It really annoyed me. I sat in my chair shaking my head, seeing the other directors wasting what I saw was precious time and money. They did not finish their scenes in the allotted time, which they seemed bewildered at, believing, as they did, that they were trying to make an artistic statement. Try doing that on a professional set, I thought, when each day of filming can cost hundreds of thousands of pounds.

The teacher then asked for another volunteer. Everyone else put their hand up to be chosen, by which time I had stood up and was already on my way to the set, ready and eager to show that I could do it. The other hands quickly went down, assuming that I had been chosen. The fact that even the teacher looked surprised as I entered the set didn't put me off one bit. I clapped my hands together, ready to get the scene in the can. Although I loved the solitude and freedom of creating, I also loved the feeling of being under pressure to produce results in a limited time. Pressure that I missed and was beginning to realize I couldn't live without for long.

I was given the scene that I had to shoot. The clock was ticking and I was off. Firstly I gave the actors their lines and sent them away to learn them. That then left me with time to go through the shots with the camera lighting and sound man. I got hold of some tape and started laying strips on the floor, each one marking the positions of the actors and cameras. Everything was in place and I was making good progress. It was time to bring on the actors who had by then learnt their lines and we were ready to shoot.

'Roll sound.'

'Sound ready.'

'Roll camera.'

'Camera ready.'

'Action!'

The camera was rolling and the adrenalin raced through my body. As each shot was completed we moved swiftly on to the next scene, trying not to lose momentum, but making sure everything was in focus and looking right as we went along.

I did everything I could to get the film in the can, and was the only one to finish within the time constraints, which was pleasing. Even with all my efficiency, however, I'd still forgotten to do the necessary close-ups for the scene. I was learning from my mistakes, as I have always done, and I was certain that it wouldn't happen again. The more I learned the more I realized there was to learn.

I thoroughly enjoyed my time at Raindance. It was hard work, but what worthwhile project isn't? By the end of the winter I had completed the first draft of my first film script and over the coming months it would be rewritten two or three more times just to fine-tune it.

I was nearly ready to move on to the next stage.

20

Helpers from the Past

I was still getting letters from the public and, as ever, I tried to answer them as best I knew how. Often I had little idea what to say to the writers, but usually I would tell them what I had done, advising them to keep looking to the future and not to remain tied up in their pasts because that would only hold them back. Then I got a letter from Ginni, the woman who befriended me through her son when I was in Yarborough children's home in East Grinstead and badly in need of an adult role model. I hadn't seen or heard from her for more than fifteen years, but I had written about her in *The Kid*, explaining the enormous help that she had been for me. She congratulated me on the book and said she wished she'd done more at the time. How could she have done more, I thought to myself, when she never realized the extent of what was going on? It seems to be a common regret amongst people that they wish they had done more in the past, and the ones who wish it the hardest always seem to be the ones who did the most in the first place.

Another letter came from Colin Smith, a teacher who I'd talked about a lot in the book because he'd done so much to help me and encourage me during the most difficult times in my life. It was Colin who had introduced me to music, which became a lifeline for me, and who had been instrumental in getting the Social Services to finally put me into a place of safety. If any one person saved me from ending up dead, he was the one. At first I didn't want to read what he had to say. I just stared at the folded letter with his name and address showing through the paper. During the writing of *The Kid* I had come to appreciate just how much this man had done for me. I knew it wasn't easy standing up to protect a child when everyone else preferred to look away, but he had. Knowing that he had read the book meant that I felt he had seen inside my head. I was apprehensive about what he might say or think about the things I had done after leaving school, the things I was less than proud of, but which I believed I had to do to get away from my past. He was someone I have an enormous amount of respect for and I did not want to feel he was disappointed in me.

Eventually I plucked up the courage and sat down to read. His letter congratulated me on the book and said how pleased he was that I'd managed to get something positive from what had happened. He also said, like Ginni, that he felt guilty he hadn't done more to follow up what happened to me after his initial intervention. I suppose everyone always regrets that they didn't do more than they did in any situation, but Colin, more than anyone, will always stand out in my memory, as he was unwilling to turn a blind eye to what he knew was going on, even when he had to tell me that things 'had to get worse before they can get better'. He stuck to his belief that something should be done, even though he was never in full possession of the facts because I kept them hidden.

It was good to know that both Colin and Ginni had read the book and seen the results of their kindness. Being a teacher in the sort of school that families like the Lewises go to must be immensely hard and usually thankless, so I hope that Colin knows how much he has achieved. I'm sure I was not the only one he has made a difference to in his career. After reading his letter I picked up the phone and called him. Even though many years had passed I immediately recognized his voice. I remembered him just as I had last seen him as a child. We spoke briefly and I suspect my voice sounded a little quiet and reserved, like a child showing respect to a teacher. We agreed to meet soon. After putting down the phone I told Jackie that I was planning to meet up with Colin again and she was encouraging. Having had time to gather my thoughts, I phoned again and invited him to the house. The day he was due to arrive I remembered the times he had helped me, refusing to give up, even after the disaster when I was asked by the social worker in front of Gloria and Dennis if I wanted to be taken into care and was too frightened to say yes.

I saw him arriving from the window and, as he got out of the car, I was amazed by how little he had changed. He had always reminded me of the actor Alan Rickman, and he still did as he walked up to the front door. He might have been a little greyer, but he was as smartly dressed as I remembered, and everything about him was co-ordinated and orderly. I'd been nervous about whether we would find anything to talk about after so long, but we sat down and immediately fell into relaxed conversation. He asked me how hard it had been to write the book, and I admitted that I had found it hard and that it had made me feel very naked, but that was the only time we mentioned it. We went out to lunch with Jackie and just chatted like old friends. I guess it must be nice for a teacher to know that he has made a difference in a pupil's life. Most of us, I imagine, leave school and don't look back, and teachers never find out how much or how little we appreciated what they did for us. I hope that we will stay in touch for ever now, as friends.

A few weeks later I received an email from the daughters of my final foster parents, Margaret and Alan, who did so much for me when I was a teenager. They had found the book in Australia and even though I'd changed their parents' names, and they were grown up and away from home by the time I was fostered, they'd still recognized their parents in the stories I told and remembered meeting me on their visits home. Alan had been the nearest thing I had to a father, but I had said some angry things in the book about the way Margaret had let me down when I was a young adult. Her daughters told me they shared my love of their father, and that they were sorry for the way Margaret had treated me after Alan had died. They also told me that Margaret had died from cancer a few months before the book was released and they advised me not to regret anything that had happened in the past, but to look to the future. I knew they were right because it was a philosophy I wholeheartedly believe in and am always saying to other people when I reply to their letters. Despite anything Margaret might have done at the end of our relationship, I felt sad that this lady who had helped so many children had passed away with such a terrible disease. I thought it appropriate to think of all the good times we had together and that is how I now and always will remember her.

Another teacher who made contact was Mrs Larkin, who was very kind to me when I was in the junior school. Firstly she pointed out that at the time she was 'Miss' Larkin, a mistake for which I apologize. She then went on to tell me that the only information she was given about me when I joined her class was that Gloria had tried to kill me with a carving knife. Although she kept an eye on me whenever I was changing for PE, she admitted, 'Gloria and Dennis were clever at hiding the bruises they inflicted.' She also admitted that I was not the only child in her class who had a difficult home life, but that she never at any stage received a visit or a call from any social workers about any of us.

'You certainly were a challenging pupil,' she went on, reminding me of one or two incidents between me and other children who had given me a hard time.

It was nice to hear back from so many people and I tried to respond as best I knew how, but I still couldn't admit to them how much my past was haunting me and how hard it was to cope with.

*

Christmas was just around the corner and I was upstairs with the kids one evening when my mobile went off and a young man introduced himself as working on behalf of the Social Services. At first I was taken aback because I was unsure what he wanted, and then I remembered my sister's children. I had put them to the back of my mind, having thought that everything had been sorted out after my discussion with their legal guardian, Carol. He was calling, he told me, with regard to those children. I wondered what had happened now as I listened, feeling a familiar and unpleasant anxiety as to what I might be about to hear.

'I've been asked to arrange a meeting with your family to see about the possibilities of you or any member of your family fostering your sister's children,' he said.

I was stunned. 'Who will be in the meeting?' I wanted to know.

'Your sister's children.'

'You mean the ones in care?' I had to confirm I'd understood him because I was having trouble believing what I was hearing.

'Yes,' he said, as if this was the most normal and sensible thing in the world.

'Who else?' I asked.

'Your sister, your mother and another sister, and I was wondering if you would come as well?'

Now I was stunned into total disbelief. After all I had been through with Carol, and having explained the situation and ensured that she understood what had happened in the past, and having been assured by her that the children would be safe and that Gloria would not be involved, we seemed to be back to square one. There I was listening to a complete stranger who was now starting the whole business again as if Carol and I had never had our conversation. Not only was he suggesting that the children should be brought into the same room with their mother and Gloria with a view to sharing them out amongst the family, he was also suggesting they went to Gloria for weekend visits. I was stunned into momentary silence and walked downstairs with the phone to my ear to listen to this guy alone, away from the children.

When I felt he had said all he had to say, which he did in the most matter-of-fact way, as if nothing unusual was being suggested, I calmly asked him what he knew of our family history. It turned out he knew nothing. The children's file had just come to the surface on his desk and he was dealing with it in complete ignorance of any of the circumstances. He knew nothing about any of us. He had only been given very limited information with which to make his decision as to how to proceed, which was why he was about to make such a colossal error of judgement. But even with such limited information I couldn't believe that he would put these young children in the same room as their abusers. He told me that he had only been given two pieces of paper with the outline of the case.

It seemed impossible to believe that in a time which is frequently referred to as the 'information age' there were still no central computer files on a family which had as bad a history as ours, that social workers would be left to stumble on in the dark, repeating the mistakes of the past over and over again. It seemed that no lessons had been learned at all. But what was most astounding about this was that the social worker who had been dealing with the case did know about our family history and had still only given this guy these few details.

I asked him if he knew anything about Gloria and he said he knew she had been hitting the children. So much frustration had been building up about this woman that I then lost it.

'Are you out of your fucking mind? Are you actually proposing to bring the children into a room with the perpetrators of their misery? What experience do you have?'

'I have a family of my own,' was his only reply.

I said I would call him back, knowing that I needed to speak with Carol, the lady who supposedly was instructed to act on behalf of the children and in their best interests. I managed to get hold of her almost immediately and explained to her my complete dismay at what was happening. She was just as flabbergasted as I was, not having been told anything about this new meeting. By the end of the call she had promised faithfully to deal with it and, true to her word, she intervened and the meeting did not take place.

For days after that I kept thinking about how disorganized the whole welfare system seems to be. Each section seems to work independently of every other one, never pulling together. What is to stop some other social worker being given the file again in a few months and being asked to sort it out without being given any more information? What security will those children ever have if they are for ever in danger of being dragged into a room with their mother and grandmother, with all the emotional strains that would put them under? The prospect of Gloria having them for weekend visits once more filled me with despair and anger. A system that was supposed to protect children was obviously filled with cracks but those in authority seemed to think everything was OK and getting better.

Carol called me back later that week and told me in no uncertain terms that Gloria would not be involved in any meeting to do with the children and assured me that the children would not be put through any such ordeal.

'That's good,' I said, 'but what about other children?'

'I can only help the ones that are assigned to me.'

It sounded as if she was as frustrated as I was. If they hadn't called me to attend the meeting; if I hadn't spoken to Carol and she hadn't got involved there would have been nothing to stop that meeting taking place. Gloria was still a potential danger to those children and I was beginning to think she might always be, until they were old enough to look after themselves.

Despite all Carol's best efforts, I couldn't rely on the fact that the system wouldn't mess up again. I knew that I had to go and see Gloria personally to tell her to stay away from children once and for all. There would now be no more imaginary glass barriers between us and I knew I had to confront her face to face for the first and final time. I was ashamed to even think that I was related to her. But I kept putting the day off. Every time I'd made up my mind to do it, I would find some pressing reason why I had to be somewhere else. I kept postponing the evil moment, again and again.

21

Travelling Back

During my time at film school we had been talking about the possibility of making a documentary about *The Kid*. I wasn't sure how I felt about the idea of going back to all the places that held such bad childhood memories, especially with the recent problems with my sister's children so raw in my mind. I'd found talking about the past to the media very difficult and so the thought of bringing it all up again made me apprehensive. The difference was I was now beginning to rebuild the barriers I had lost and, to be honest, when the idea came up there was a part of me that was curious about what it would feel like to return. I also began to wonder if physically going back to my past could help me finally put it to rest in my mind. In a slightly sick way I wanted to find out how I would react to going back, although the thought of doing it in front of a camera made me nervous.

Because we had a few people interested I was able to choose a company I felt comfortable with. I didn't want to do anything that was just about the past and wallow in how miserable it all was; I wanted the documentary to look to the future and be hopeful and encouraging to anyone who was watching, just as I had hoped the book had been.

We looked at the various proposals and the best option came from the BBC, who wanted to talk to me and some of my brothers and sisters and also to people like Ginni and Colin Smith. What amazed me was that during the BBC's research for the documentary I found out that Colin had kept detailed records on me when I was a child, noting occasions when I collapsed in the playground after having had a beating at home and other events which I'd thought nobody had noticed. It felt strange to discover that someone else had been watching over me so closely without me realizing and that he still had those records of what he saw. He declined to appear in front of the cameras, being a very private man, but gave them access to the information he had gathered.

I agreed to go ahead with the programme and one of the things that the director wanted to do was go back to the pink tin house in New Addington. The idea of going back made me feel physically sick with anxiety, a mixture of thoughts and feelings that made me very uncomfortable and worried about what I might see. It was obvious that they would ask me to go back to the house as it was a major part of my childhood and I tried to prepare myself mentally. Jackie noticed that I was extremely agitated once more and when they gave me the date of the trip about a week before, I began to get nightmares again. I don't remember what they were about, but I would wake at around one or two o'clock in the morning in a pool of sweat, unable to get back to sleep because all my senses were alert. I would go downstairs and work until morning.

It wasn't the first time I'd been back to New Addington

since escaping from home. I had walked around the area when I was writing *The Kid*, to remind myself of the layout and the atmosphere, but I hadn't felt brave enough to knock on the door of the house and ask to see inside. The best I could do was to drive past with it just in sight, unable to actually turn into the Horseshoe. I'd been up to the market where I'd worked as a young boy and bought a packet of chips and some fruit and vegetables, which had brought back some pleasant memories of my first tentative steps towards independence. Then I drove away again, back to the safety of my new life. I tried really hard to prepare myself, wanting to prove I was strong and no longer fearful of the past, but deep down I wasn't sure how I would react to crossing the threshold of the house that held so many terrible memories.

As always seems to happen when I am about to do something related to my past, I didn't sleep at all the night before we were due to go filming. It was a long night, my mind running around in circles about what I would see when I got there. Even though I was now a grown man with the security of a loving family, I knew I still felt as vulnerable as a small boy at the thought of stepping back inside that house later that day. As the night dragged on it angered me that I could still be made to feel like this after so long. I told myself that this would be the last time I would ever have to go back inside the house and once I'd got through this day I would never have to think about it again and I tried to convince myself that I would have gained some sort of closure on my past by making this final trip.

The director and producer wanted to film me inside the tin house on the first day, which we all agreed was best because it would then be out the way. I didn't want to have to do all the other filming with that hanging over me.

It was a cold, rainy winter's day as we set off slowly from my new life to my previous life. As we got closer, I grew more nervous. To break me in gently on the day of filming, I was first taken to the woods at the end of the road, which I used to run away to when I was tiny. They hadn't changed at all. People might come and go, the children of the area might grow up and leave home, but the landscape evolved at its own slow pace, bringing back a hundred memories of me as a small boy running as far away from Gloria and Dennis as possible. I could even find the slope that I used to slide down to get into the cover of the undergrowth quickly when I was in a hurry to disappear, and I wondered if other children used it in the same way as I had, keeping it smooth and well-worn. I remembered the times when I went back home, too scared to stay in the woods any longer, but still terrified to step into the house. As I walked slowly back across the grass in the middle of the Horseshoe I would know that she would be watching me from the window. Before I even reached the garden path the door would be thrown open and Gloria would be standing there, staring down, fag in mouth, ordering me to get inside in a tone that told me what was going to happen as soon as the door was closed against prying eyes. The moment it shut behind me chaos would ensue and everything I had been imagining on the long walk home would happen. The pain of those beatings would stay with me for days afterwards.

At the end of King Henry's Drive, opposite the woods, the tower blocks that I used to run past in my desperate bids for freedom had had a facelift since I'd last been there. The grey pebble-dash walls were now beige, and the window frames had been painted red, making the tower blocks look slightly less forbidding. The goal posts stood in the same place as they had twenty years earlier on the open grass area leading into the woods. As I walked through the woods I noticed that they didn't seem as big now as I remembered. I suppose things all look much larger when you are a small child. But one thing only was on my mind as we strolled around, and that was the pink tin house.

As we drove down from the woods in our wet clothes to the Horseshoe, the crescent where the house stood back from King Henry's Drive, my pulse began to quicken and the butterflies started their familiar war dance in my stomach. The road looked exactly the same as I remembered apart from the red telephone box that had once stood in the centre and had now disappeared. The cars parked in front of the houses were more modern, but otherwise time had stood still. It seemed strange that when so much had changed in my life, so little had changed here.

The family who now live in the pink tin house had read the book and were happy to let us come in and film. I wondered how many other people in the neighbourhood had read what I had written.

I drove past at a virtual snail's pace, my eyes glued to

the house. I parked the car and sat in full sight of the pink tin walls, just staring at it. The net curtains were blocking anyone from looking inside, just as they had when I lived there. Before I got out of the car I tried to compose myself. It was time to confront my demons, I said to myself. I got out and approached the front door, and as I slowly walked up to the house I felt that each step was making me smaller. All my senses were on alert like a wild animal treading cautiously for fear of walking into a trap. I could feel the blood pumping round my body. As my eyes flickered around I noticed that the paint was flaking on top of the metal porch, just as it was all those years before.

As I was getting closer, I was having difficulty rationalizing everything that was going on around me. I tried to keep my breathing steady and not panic and for some reason my mind was blank. I couldn't think of anything. The front door was wide open, but I wasn't ready to go in yet. Instead I stayed at the side of the porch unable to face the entrance directly, peering round the corner, like a frightened rabbit on the edge of a road. All my muscles were shaking with nerves now, my instincts telling me I should turn and run. I tried to consciously calm them down, but there was nothing I could do. All I could do was tell myself not to run away.

I kept dipping my toe into the waters; poking my head round for a few seconds to look and then pulling it back out and taking a deep breath, as if trying to convince myself it was all right to venture the final few steps out of a safe hiding place. Suddenly I burst out crying, my shoulders heaving, unable to control the feelings of what had gone on inside those tin walls as the memories rushed over me. I tried to stand up straight and get control, telling myself that I was better than this, that I could do it.

I could feel that I wasn't ready yet to take the plunge; that I needed a little longer to get used to the idea. I went back to the car to get my sunglasses, wanting to have something to hide behind, something to cover my nakedness. My legs were shaking uncontrollably and threatening to buckle under me at any moment as I attempted to enter the house once again. I was trying to focus my thoughts, but my whole mind was taken up with the task of overcoming my fears so that I could at least step through the door. I felt physically sick.

Eventually, mustering all my courage, my sunglasses giving me the barrier I needed, I cautiously put one leg through the door and then stopped again before following with the other one, taking my reluctant body into the house. As I came into the hallway I couldn't stop the tears from coming and I was grateful to have the protection of the glasses. I still felt physically sick, but at least I was inside. I'd taken the plunge. Someone went to close the door behind me, but I told them to leave it open, feeling a surge of panic. I had to know that I could get out at any moment. I couldn't take the chance of feeling trapped inside the house ever again. I was trying not to breathe too deeply, frightened that if I did I might catch a whiff of some smell that would bring back pictures of my childhood even more vividly. I had to be able to filter the memories that I allowed through, for fear that I would be overwhelmed by them.

The first thing I noticed as I stood in the hallway was that the kitchen door had been blocked off. I could picture how it had been to look through and see the sink full of dirty dishes and me being washed in full view of the school that we backed on to. I could still recall the smoky, greasy smell that would always linger on my body after being strip-washed in the sink water.

It took me almost as long to get from the doorway into the first room as it had taken to get through the front door. I kept bobbing my head round the corner, as if wanting to be absolutely sure there was nobody waiting to pounce before I would go any deeper into the house. Even though my body didn't want to go any further, my mind was curious to see what the rooms looked like now. As I went into the front room I noticed that the door between the room I stood in and the dining room was no longer there, which gave a clear view to the garden at the back. I noticed it was clean and well tended with a new decking area and a familiar view of Wolsey Junior School. I could hear the sound of children playing in the playground and as I walked closer to the window I could see them happily running around in their break. My eyes scanned the garden more closely. It was no longer the overgrown rubbish tip of my youth, but a family garden full of children's toys.

As I started to focus through my tears I could see that the inside of the house was also a hundred times cleaner and neater than when we lived there. I saw the corner I used to hide in while watching TV with filth surrounding me on the floor and clothes piled high against the wall like a jumble sale. I would hide amongst the clothes to keep out of the way of Gloria and Dennis and they also helped keep me warm.

As I walked from the dining room into the kitchen I remembered how my feet would stick to the floor and how when I got up from sitting on the floor my legs would be covered in filth and my feet were permanently black. The hardest time to get used to it was after having returned from the clean environment of Yarborough Children's Home. I could picture the time when Dennis threw the carving knife at Wayne and the feeling of nausea grew stronger as other images crowded in behind it. The worktop behind the kitchen door where Dennis used to stand, hour after hour, drinking and listening to Elvis songs, was still in the same place it had always been, the sink was still beneath the window where passers-by used to be able to see us being strip-washed in the most humiliating fashion, but the outside toilet had been converted into something else.

Although I managed to force myself to look round the downstairs, I couldn't bring myself to go upstairs and risk meeting all the ghosts that would be lying in wait for me. The visions of Gloria in the room and what she would do to me were just too painful. I knew that once up in those rooms, I would be too far from the open front door and I was sure I would panic. I stayed inside for as long as I could bear it.

'I want to go home now,' I said.

I'd had enough. My brain was racing at a hundred miles an hour. I felt as if I wanted to smash my head against the tin wall just to get rid of all the visions that had been in there for so long. Instead, I tasted blood in my mouth from where I had been biting my lip too hard. Once outside I took a deep lungful of fresh air. That was it, I thought to myself as I headed for the car. I'd done it and there was no way I was ever going to be going back in there.

The owners of the house had tactfully gone out to give the film crew freedom to move about, but the three adult daughters had stayed upstairs out of the way. I went back to meet them at the front of the house not long after, my sunglasses still on to hide my swollen eyes. I thanked them for letting me back into the house. I realized that they were lovely people and that no matter what happened when I lived there they had a different life in that house, a life that seemed a million miles away from mine. They said that if I ever wanted to go back inside they wouldn't have a problem. I kindly thanked them for their offer and said that I could never do that. They seemed to understand. Finally they gave me a bottle of wine, which I thought was a lovely gesture. We said our goodbyes and as I drove away, leaving the house behind me, I knew I would never return. It was a past life and I had finally buried it.

One of the girls from the pink tin house was a cleaner at Wolsey Junior and she very kindly took me around to the school so I could see what had changed. Apart from the entrance hall it all looked completely different, unlike the house. Although Wolsey Junior didn't hold any happy memories, it didn't have the same dramatic effect on me as the house had done.

I found out afterwards that in their research the film crew had found a number of neighbours and people in the area who knew what was going on in that house. They all said they wished they had done more, but were too frightened to help for fear of retaliation from Gloria and Dennis. One was an elderly lady, in one of the other houses on the Horseshoe, called Iris. I didn't remember her, but she remembered me and also said she had realized what had been going on. She thought I had got the worst of it because I had often been the one to stick up for myself and for the others. Iris was a nice woman and she told me she was still in touch with one of my sisters. The day was over and that night I slept more peacefully than I had for ages, safe in the knowledge that I would never have to return.

The following day we went back to Yarborough children's home, which had been converted into a nursery school and flats. As I stood outside I felt much more relaxed than I had done when I visited the pink tin house and even began joking around in front of the camera. These had been relatively happy times for me. I could see the window through which we tried to run away after watching *Huckleberry Finn*. I could see the big white door where I was first greeted by Uncle David, a giant of a man, and where he later got on his knees to say goodbye as I was taken back to the tin house.

The documentary makers wanted to interview me further, but I wasn't keen on the idea of putting myself through the whole thing again as I felt uneasy showing my vulnerability on camera. But then I agreed to go ahead, deciding that as each part of the filming was finished I would be able to put that part of my life behind me. I felt as if I was building a wall bit by bit, adding layer after layer of cement so that it wouldn't come down again if anything else happened in the Lewis family.

I didn't want to do the interview at home, I wanted to feel more detached, and so I asked if we could film it in a neutral place. As they asked their questions I began to describe things that had happened in the tin house, both to me and in front of me. For the first time I spoke out loud about some of the things that happened and I actually felt better after it; but I knew I didn't want to talk about it ever again.

After that the director thought it would be nice to have a section with me and Wayne hanging out together at the pub, playing pool together. I wasn't comfortable with the idea since we never did anything like that and it wouldn't be natural.

'Could we do an activity together?' I suggested, thinking that the novelty value of learning something new would take our minds off the more emotional parts of the meeting. 'How about fly fishing?'

I don't know why I suggested that since Wayne had never done fly fishing in his life and I'd only done it twice before, but I thought it would be fun. The director agreed and we all headed off to a nearby lake. Wayne and I got some practice in while the camera crew were setting themselves up and he immediately caught a huge fish, but the cameras weren't ready and missed the whole event. Once they were up and running we didn't get a single bite all afternoon. In the end the owner of the fish farm allowed us to go to the feeding pond, where it's almost impossible not to catch something. Wayne managed another triumph and couldn't help but take the mickey out of me for my failure to catch a single fish.

Later that evening Wayne was interviewed; I stayed in the room next door just in case he needed me for support. After his interview, which I could see had upset him, we put our arms around each other and held on tightly. It was something we had both wanted to do for a long time. Later that evening we went out together, just the two of us, for the first time since we were children. While we were out I saw some friends and felt so proud to be able to introduce my brother to them.

Talking about the past with Wayne was emotional. He told me that since reading the book he had managed to get better control of his temper and wasn't as defensive towards people as he had been and he felt that as a result of this he had been promoted at work. I felt so pleased for him and was so proud of his achievement that it was almost as though it was me getting the promotion, until he told me to calm down.

On the last day of filming Jackie was interviewed and the kids were filmed playing with us. The smiles on our faces were real that day because it was all behind us and I was now in my new life with a wonderful caring wife and two fantastic children who meant the world to both of us.

All that was left was to confront Gloria in order to tell her to leave the children alone, but now I also wanted to see Dennis, not for the same reason, but because I wanted to know that I was no longer afraid of the past.

Just before the programme was aired the BBC wrote

to Gloria and Dennis explaining what they were doing and asking whether they would like to comment. There was no response from Dennis and we didn't expect one from Gloria either, as Wayne had already asked if she would be interviewed, an invitation she had declined. After receiving the letter, however, she contacted the producer and agreed to be interviewed. When I heard of her decision I felt nothing. She knew what went on all those years ago and I felt curious as to how she would justify it and what she would say.

At the end of the filming I was due to go to Argentina. The producer told me that upon my return I would receive a copy of the documentary before it was aired to the public. I was going to have to wait until then to find out what Gloria said. Even though I knew in my heart that I had to confront her – to tell her to stay away from the children once and for all – I still wanted to put the moment of the meeting off. Having just relived my past so painfully, I decided to leave that task until my return, when I would feel more relaxed emotionally and ready to face anything.

22

Argentina

Martin, my first polo coach, had suggested that if I really wanted to improve my game, particularly my riding style, then I should spend some time in Argentina where he also spends part of his year. I was to stay at La Esperanza Polo Club in the town of Coronel Suarez, which is known as the world capital of polo and is where some of the best players in the world have come from. Having never had any proper training I knew that if I wanted to progress I needed to work on my riding skills, so I booked to go over to La Esperanza for ten days at the end of January.

This would be the longest period I had ever been away from Jackie or the kids, and the first time I had ever travelled abroad on my own. I didn't like the idea of being apart from them but I thought this was too good an opportunity to miss. Jackie and I had spent so much time together over the previous year and had so much fun that I felt I could justify it.

As the day of departure drew closer, however, I became increasingly unhappy at the thought of leaving them behind for such a long time. I kept telling myself that it was only for ten days, but the feeling of sadness just wouldn't go away, partly because as a family we are so close and have so much quality time together and partly because I was nervous about how I would fit in to the life of the family who ran the club and who would be my hosts for the stay. I am always completely comfortable with my own loving family around me and the idea of leaving them behind made me feel both guilty and anxious.

Eventually the day of departure came round and the taxi turned up at the house on a cold, drizzly Saturday evening to take me to Heathrow for the night flight. By this time I really didn't want to leave the warmth and comfort of a family weekend together and it wouldn't have taken much for me to stay. But Jackie thought that after all that had happened recently it would do me the world of good. She had packed my bag and made sure I had all the necessary travel documents. There was no turning back. As I left I felt so bad as a father to be leaving them all, especially on such a dreary night.

I hadn't wanted Jackie to come to the airport with me because I thought the goodbyes would be too difficult, especially with the children and with this being our first time apart. When I got to the terminal I realized how much I had grown to rely on Jackie over the years. Not only would I not have been able to organize myself in time for the departure from home, I knew that I would most probably have forgotten all the documentation. Even when I got to the airport I wasn't able to find where I had to be and ended up in the wrong queue. A British Airways member of staff had to take me and lead me through the departure process, which was a little embarrassing, to say the least, but very appreciated as I handed the lady all my paperwork and she sifted through it to find the necessary bits and pieces for me to fly. I already missed Jackie and the kids desperately as I waited for the flight to be announced.

Once on board, I settled into my seat awaiting take-off. We were up in the air in no time, ploughing through the wet and windy evening as I watched the wings flapping around with some discomfort. Eventually I fell asleep and arrived in Buenos Aires over fifteen hours later, feeling uncomfortable from the flight.

I was met at the airport by Carlitos who was a member of the Bertola family, who owned La Esperanza. The polo club was over five hundred kilometres away, just outside the town of Coronel Suarez, South West towards the mountainous region of Ventana. He greeted me warmly and spoke good English. We soon started making conversation and I realized I should have taken some time to learn a few words of Spanish. I told Carlitos that I spoke no Spanish and apologized for my ignorance. He didn't mind as he was happy to practise his English on me and in return he taught me a few basic phrases so that at least I could greet people and thank them.

As we set off on the four-hour drive to the club the air was already humid and the ground steaming from the night's rainfall. We soon settled in to the long drive ahead of us. The distance seemed like nothing to him as he made the trip to the capital regularly, but it was a hell of a long way for me. What amazed me as we drove at what you might politely call a progressive speed was the sheer scale and beauty of the scenery. It was so flat you could see the open lush farmland for miles in every direction. After three and a half hours of driving on completely flat roads, with not much else to look at except the odd passing vehicle, I noticed a small gradient up ahead and I found myself looking forward to the change. I tried to make a joke about it to Carlitos, which fell flat on its face when I had to explain it to him for the third time. Carlitos smiled politely, probably wondering who the hell he had got sitting in the car next to him. As we reached our destination I could clearly see the spectacular Ventana mountains in the background.

Martin and the whole Bertola family, including the father and mother, their sons, daughters, sons-in-law and grandchildren, all came out to greet me. They were so warm and welcoming that I couldn't help but feel truly comfortable in their home. The accommodation con-sisted of a number of villas, all very European in style, which housed guests like me and other players who had travelled from all over the world. The villas were divided up into cool, elegant apartments with wooden floors and windows which looked out across the open farmland where over two hundred polo ponies grazed and worked in rotation. The sweet smell of newly mown grass floated on the breeze, filtered by the mosquito nets that guarded each open window. It was a very pleasant and peaceful farm and I couldn't have asked for more. Jose Bertola, a five-goal player, was going to be my instructor during my time there, along with Martin who was going to be helping me improve my riding. They were such genu-inely pleasant people, and their willingness to try to communicate with me in English when I had no Spanish to offer in return was a relief, although I did feel a little stupid. All I had were the few words Carlitos had taught me, of which I can now remember only 'Hola' and 'Gracias'. They asked what I wanted to do and I couldn't hold back my eagerness to get out on to the polo pitch. They were more than happy to oblige and I soon settled into a very relaxed and chilled routine.

Breakfast would be served at nine thirty in the morning. After that I would have my riding lessons to try to get myself sitting properly in the saddle, not pulling so much on the ponies' mouths or kicking their bellies so hard, just settling in and being more at one with my mounts and not riding with chicken arms and bicycle legs. The mornings' activities would help me work up a healthy appetite for the mighty family lunches, which would lead to everyone having a siesta during the hottest hours of the day in order, I think, to rest their swollen stomachs. If I couldn't sleep I would sit under the shade of the willow trees that surrounded the swimming pool and write in my black book, read or doze.

Sometimes I would come inside and sit in front of the television in the guest lounge, watching videos of the professional players, trying to take in their techniques. I would wait impatiently for five thirty to arrive, when the heat of the sun would begin to relent and we would play chukkas late into the evening.

I soon began to slow down from the frantic pace of life in England. I took off my watch because I wanted to move at their relaxed, chilled pace, which evaporated as soon as we started to play chukkas. Then the whole place came alive with players arriving from all over the area, all of them very skilled. There I would be playing twenty-goal practice chukkas with these very talented players. It felt great and was like mixing with Premier Division footballers, people at the top of their game. At first I felt completely out of my depth, but they knew I wanted to learn and helped me a great deal. It was tiring work, making my inside legs burn from the effort of staying on the ponies, something the other players seemed to do effortlessly in a style I was keen to learn.

After chukkas we would have another rest before the evening meal, which was served in the big house. This was a time when all the family and anyone else who was staying at the club would come together. The food was fabulous, and we ate a lot of esados, which were various meats that they cooked slowly over hot charcoal for hours, making the meat as soft as jelly in the mouth. They were so hospitable and nothing was too much trouble. It was during the meals, as I watched all the different generations mixing together, laughing and enjoying one another's company, that I missed Jackie and the kids the most. Being slightly on the outside gave me an opportunity to observe and think, and it made me realize what a great family life I had back at home. They would ask me about my family and I would eagerly tell them about Jackie and the children. They would all listen attentively, and I told them how the love I had for my family was just like the love they had for theirs.

As my morning lessons progressed I began learning to control and understand the ponies better. Martin was taking time to ride alongside me and I was becoming less nervous when they threw their heads around, became agitated or behaved differently from one another. I was finding out that they all had different personalities, just like people, and you had to respect them. Some were grumpy while others were eager to please, some were leaders, others followers. Some of them would be able to tell that I wasn't an experienced rider, while others didn't seem to notice. By the end of the ten days I had ridden over forty different ponies and my confidence had grown immeasurably. The Argentinians had shown me how important these ponies were to the sport, and how much respect they deserved. These responsive creatures are the finest sporting animals in the world, having to be as fast as racehorses and as agile and powerful as boxers. I also found that the spectators were just as interested in the ponies as the players, and this made sense to me as the ponies made up over seventy five per cent of the game. I realized that whereas before I had treated all the ponies the same, as machines, I was now looking at them with far more respect and this gave me an added understanding and more confidence in my riding.

Jose was teaching me to focus more tightly on what was happening all around me on the pitch in order to keep up with the others and anticipate where the game was going, rather than just charging around all the time in an uncontrollable gallop. I had to concentrate hard.

I was learning fast and I began to predict for myself where to aim the ball, rather than just whacking it as hard as I could and it going nowhere. I felt that these new skills were not only helping me to discipline myself in the game but also helping with other things as well. I found that by focusing on the game I was doing the same as I was with my family life. The more I was in control of my vivid childhood visions, the more I seemed to be able to filter out those that were of no use to me now. Jose was teaching me that if I made a mistake or committed a foul in the game I didn't have to worry about it, just try and learn from it and get on with the game. A skill that is true in any walk of life. One of the most frequent errors made by a new player is to worry about not fouling, or making a mistake and letting it get you down – another truth in life as well as in sport. The foul or mistake is in the past, so leave it there. Learn from it and move on, more experienced and wiser because of it. Whereas I had always panicked about every error I made, I realized these professionals also made mistakes, but they never dwelled on them. I now firmly believe that learning a new sport helps to develop you in ways you never imagine both in your mind and in your attitude to life.

I was so fascinated by my new-found sport that some evenings, when the others suggested we go out into the town, I would decline, wanting to get an early night so that I was fresh for the next day. On the nights I did go out we would go to a local bar in the historical town of Coronel Suarez, with its beautiful buildings and cobbled streets and I would find myself mixing with some of the top professional polo players in the world. They were so warm, friendly and happy that I was learning their sport. It felt like having a drink with Michael Owen and David Beckham and once again I felt in awe of the game and of the passion of the people who played it.

One night we all went to visit another family in the area. I was a little apprehensive, knowing that they would all be old friends and I would be the outsider, and painfully aware of the language barrier. I needn't have worried: they were as hospitable as the Bertolas and spoke perfect English, which made me feel even more ashamed at my lack of linguistic abilities. I promised myself that I would learn more for my next trip over, which I was already thinking about, except next time I planned to bring my family. At the end of an evening of wonderful food and hospitality under the stars, they produced a worn old leather visitors' book and asked me if I would sign it. As I rested this worn book on my lap I opened it gently and looked at the pages of comments that went back nearly forty years in every conceivable language, all made by previous visitors to their home. I couldn't think of anything to write apart from thanking them for a wonderful evening in a wonderful home with a wonderful family, which seemed to sum up my views of the whole trip. Unfortunately I spelled 'wonderful' wrong, but I could always blame the wine. It reminded me of our dream home – a traditional farmhouse with timber frames inside, and big open fireplaces giving off a smoky smell. I have always found smoky smells comforting ever since being rescued from the pink house by a fireman. Our dream house will have its own life and character and we will spend the rest of our lives there, settled and happy. I knew that once we got our home I would have a book like the one resting on my lap, a book of sincerity that would last for generations.

It made me realize just how much I missed and appreciated my family.

I phoned home regularly and towards the end of the trip Jackie told me that a video of the documentary had arrived and that she had watched it. She said it had made her cry. I didn't ask about the interview with Gloria as I no longer wanted her in my head, obstructing my new life.

After dinner one evening the family asked me what I wrote about when I was sitting by the pool and for the first time ever I agreed to show other people what was in my black book and the storyboards for the film and the novel I was creating, as well as my inventions. As I returned from my room with the black book under my arm they all crowded round, curious to see what I spent hours by the pool doing. It didn't matter that some of them didn't speak any English; they could understand what I was getting at just by looking at the pages. Their eyes would light up as I explained my stories and inventions late into the night, and they listened intently and asked questions through Carlitos, their chosen interpreter. It was the first time I had ever let anyone look at these pages, not even Jackie had seen them, and I must admit I felt proud to show them.

Just as those ten days in Argentina had helped me to focus even more clearly on my life and my ambitions, they had also given me a chance to work out what I should do about my parents. I had already decided I was going to have to go to see them. As I was always the one who had tried to stand up to them it was time for me to stand up to them again, especially Gloria, and tell her that she couldn't have anything more to do with any children; that she simply couldn't be trusted not to hurt them any longer.

On my last night at La Esperanza I had a vivid dream. Jackie, the children and I were all living back in the pink tin house that I had been brought up in. We were there because I was a Lewis and it was the Lewis family home. The authorities had arrived unannounced to take the children away from us and into care. The kids were screaming for us as the social workers hauled them off by their arms, pulling hard and I was being held back as I desperately fought for my children. They were being taken away because we were part of the Lewis family and we had all been tarnished with the same brush as Gloria. Then the dream changed and at the end of the table sat a judge. The children were next to the social workers, their arms being held tightly so they couldn't move. The social workers looked at them and us with arrogant expressions. We were all crying, trying to plead for the children to be with us, saying that we had done nothing wrong. Then the judge looked at the social workers with disgust, ordering them to take their hands off the children. As soon as they were released the kids ran towards us and I was jerked awake, covered in a cold sweat. The sheets were soaked as if I had wet the bed, my heart thumping hard.

I was sure the dream had been brought on by the nerves I was feeling at the prospect of confronting Gloria. I knew I had to do it for the sake of the children and I also knew I needed to find some sort of closure for myself in my relationship with her, but that didn't make the prospect of seeing her any less frightening.

Martin and I left later that day to spend an evening in Buenos Aires before my flight home. I said my goodbyes, vowing to return with my family. I especially thanked Jose for all his help in teaching me about the ponies and the game. Knowing I had learned so much more about myself and about dealing with life, I gave a special thanks to his father whose company I had enjoyed so much. I was sad to leave but eager to return to my own family.

When I arrived home I gave Jackie a huge hug and we clung tightly to each other. We collected the kids from school together and we were all excited to be a family once more.

Later that evening I sat down and watched the documentary. Out of everything the one thing that surprised me the most was that during the course of filming they had filmed upstairs in the old tin house and the current family had shown them some of the original scribbles they had found on those filthy walls, now hidden by a wardrobe. The camera had panned in and clearly made out the words 'Help me'. It didn't bother me so much now as finally I saw myself in that room again with no pane of glass. I could see Gloria walking out the door, not even turning to look at me and I was finally left alone to get on with my dreams.

As the interview of Gloria came on, it was obvious that she still didn't believe she had done anything wrong. But what I hadn't known was that her father had beaten her when she was a child. She said she believed that it was normal back then to do what she did to me. But what about what was happening today, I thought. She told the camera I was 'a little terror' as a child and therefore had needed to be disciplined. Finally she said that if she did it all again she would only have two children. As I sat and watched, the thought of the programme going out to millions of people didn't make me feel as naked as the idea of the book had done. It seemed that I had managed to move on and by the end it looked as though it would be possible to get the closure I wanted if I just faced up to my past once and for all – which meant going to see Gloria and Dennis.

I had to do it for the sake of the children, and I had to do it for myself as well. Over the years I had always concentrated on getting myself as far as possible from the brutality and misery of my childhood, determined to work hard and be the best husband and father I could possibly be. I knew I'd done well and had a wonderful life now, but I still had a few more demons that lurked in my memory and my subconscious. Writing the book had been the only sort of therapy I had ever indulged in and it had stirred up too many memories and realizations for comfort. I now wanted to find some sort of closure to the whole business of that part of my life. I would only find that by going to face my parents.

As I thought about what I had to do next I had no idea how Gloria would react to me when I turned up on the doorstep, whether she would physically attack me for what I'd written in *The Kid* or whether she would pretend there was nothing wrong between us and never had been.

23

Dennis

My decision to go and see Dennis was taken as much out of curiosity than anything else. The last time I'd spoken to him was when he had ended the conversation by telling me he loved me and I hadn't known how to react to the one gesture I had been so desperate for as a child. His words had been coming back to me a great deal since then and I felt I needed to go and see him in order to work out how I felt about him and about the role he had played in my childhood and in my life now.

I knew from Robert and the girls that he was poorly, but I had no idea what to expect. I didn't know if he would be pleased to see me or not. If I hadn't embarked on writing *The Kid* and unlocked all the memories, I'm not sure I ever would have seen him again.

A few days after getting back from Argentina I drove up to his flat in the morning, straight after dropping the children off at school. I thought he was less likely to have taken a drink at that time of day and I would be able to avoid all the emotional outpourings that came when his inhibitions were removed by alcohol. I hadn't actually seen him face to face for over seven years and I knew that during that time he had changed his lifestyle from visiting the local pubs, as he had when I was a child, to becoming a virtual recluse. I remembered those long days in the pubs, where he would just sit, nursing a drink at the bar, exchanging the odd word or two with a familiar face, while I sat in the corner, waiting for him to decide it was time to go home, relieved to be out of the house and away from Gloria. Now he didn't even have that much company in his life.

Did he really love me? Or had that just been the drink talking? If he did mean it, how should I respond? I had a feeling that he might now need me more than I needed him. The time when I had really needed him to rescue me was as a child, but so many times he would turn into a raging bull, so full of anger and egged on by Gloria. After so many years of him inflicting horrific punishments on me out of all proportion to any crime I might have committed, part of me could see no reason why I should do anything to help him now. If I was to forgive him, then that would mean I was saying what he did was OK.

The man who had been a real father figure for me was Alan, my foster father in the few years before I was left to my own devices. I wasn't sure that I had room to let Dennis back into my life on a regular basis. I wasn't sure if I should feel any sort of responsibility to look after him if he needed it or not, or how he would react to Jackie and his grandchildren.

I knew that I lived such a different life from Dennis now and I wasn't sure he could be part of it or where he would fit in, especially with his drinking which could trigger his temper and drunken outpourings of self-pitying emotion. I could never let my children be subjected to that. So many terrible things had happened in that house when he was the adult and I was the child, it wasn't possible to just put them all to one side and say everything would be all right between us now. But was I being selfish to the children who might like to see their granddad? All they knew of the past was that Daddy's parents weren't nice to him. They didn't know the extent of how he had behaved towards me. To them he would just be an old man who might love them. He was, after all, my father, and now he was ill. Robert had told me he had suffered from three strokes and his arthritis was getting worse. It seemed likely to me that the drink was killing him. If only he could stop, I said to myself, but then I thought, what has he got to stop for?

I drove to the cream-coloured building in south London that housed his flat and I was surprised to find that I didn't feel that nervous, not like I knew I would feel when I finally got round to confronting Gloria. It was a ground-floor apartment with its own front door at the top of a short flight of steps. I knocked. He wasn't expecting me. I didn't call ahead in case he said he didn't want to see me. He opened the door wearing a white shirt and suit trousers, as if he was halfway through getting dressed for going to work in an office somewhere. His sleeves were rolled up and his arms looked sore and scabby. His hair was a big greyer than I remembered, but he hadn't changed much apart from that; he was still the stocky man I always remembered.

'Hi,' I said, awkwardly.

'Oh, hello,' he replied, in his usual shy manner, standing back to let me into the clean but musty-smelling rooms. He didn't register any great surprise at seeing me.

The small flat comprised of a kitchen, a lounge and a bedroom. I could imagine how claustrophobic it must have seemed when Robert was staying there too, spending his nights on the sofa. It was no wonder they'd fallen out with one another. There were no family pictures anywhere but the walls were covered with pictures and posters of Elvis. Even the mirror had 'the King's' face printed on it.

Everything was stained yellow from the endless clouds of smoke emitted from Dennis's endlessly lit cigarettes. The air smelled as if it hadn't been changed for a long time and I didn't like having to breathe it. I thought of the years he had spent smoking away while he drank himself into his rages. His kitchen was sparse and it didn't look like there was much food there. Even though he was hobbling along as he had always done it was obvious that he was a lot weaker than I remembered. Every so often he would burst into a coughing fit, keeping his mouth closed so that his face turned bright red, just as it used to when I was a child. I didn't want to sit down, so I hovered uncomfortably, not sure if I was a welcome guest or a trespasser, unable to think of any topics of conversation that didn't sound forced and false.

'I heard you wrote a book,' he said at one moment and I nodded, but he didn't ask any more.

'How are you getting on?' I asked, feeling a heavy weight of depression descending on my chest.

He seemed such a sad figure, to have started life by being taken into care and then to have spent so many years drinking and smoking and trying in vain to think of some way to escape from the stress of his marriage and the endless children under his feet. In a way he had found an escape in this depressing little flat, but it seemed the horrors of being trapped with Gloria had been replaced with the horrors of his own company, with Elvis once again his only means of escape.

I couldn't imagine that he had any memories that he could look back on with fondness, no achievements that he could feel proud of, as he sat smoking listening to the King. It was as if he was simply existing, marking time until the drink finished him off. It all seemed such a terrible waste of a life.

I told him that the kids were growing up and going to school and he nodded, with his cigarette in the corner of his mouth, to show that he had taken in the information, but he didn't ask anything about them.

'Are you going to sit down then?' he enquired, with the hint of a mocking smile. I sat, even though I would have preferred to remain standing.

Once or twice, amongst the uncomfortable pauses, he tried to smile at me but it seemed as if living on his own, not going to the pub any more and having little interaction with others had made him even less able to communicate with his fellow man. I couldn't think of anything to say to ease the tension between us.

'Do you need any help?' I asked eventually and he shook his head.

In the uncomfortable silence I began to tell him what I was up to now. I told him I was writing more. I explained about film school, the inventions and everything else that I was trying to achieve. As I sat next to him I became excited about telling him what I was achieving, like I thought a son should proudly tell his father. I explained what my life was like with Jackie and the children and my arms were waving about as I continued to describe my passions. But then I stopped and looked at him. I just wanted a reaction from him. Deep down I really wanted to know if he did care; that would be a start, I thought, but his head just kept nodding in a lifeless way, the smoke curling upwards towards the stained ceiling. I tried to tell him about his grandchildren, but he didn't seem interested. Before I went into the flat I wasn't sure how he would fit into our lives and now I was there I still didn't know how I felt. He just didn't seem bothered.

I doubt if I was in there for more than twenty minutes. At one point I went to put my hand on his shoulder, but I thought better of it. I had a feeling that even a small physical gesture like that might unleash the most terrible flood of emotions which neither of us would be able to cope with. I knew I had been his favourite from little things he had said and done over the years, sometimes just the odd passing look in the middle of some family battle scene or other. I also knew that some of the stress between him and Gloria had been caused by their very different feelings for me. But if he had loved me, then he should have saved me. The fact that he just didn't seem interested now was very depressing. I was trying my hardest to communicate with him, but it was all in vain. We said our goodbyes, not touching each other, and Dennis closed the door as soon as I had gone down a few steps.

As I came away I felt really down and wondered whether I had done the right thing in writing about this fragile man who had tried to work hard but just hadn't been able to cope with all the pressures around him. Was it his fault if he just wasn't up to the job of having a family?

I didn't cry when I got back into the car, but I was lost in thought all the way home. I tried to think of the times when he would take me to the pub with him as a child. Dennis would be drinking at the bar and I would be sat in the corner on the old leather sofas, out of the way, with an orange squash in front of me, happy at the thought of being out of the house for a while, safely away from Gloria.

I didn't feel like doing much else that day, just sat around, trying to work out how I felt and, more importantly, how he felt. I came to the conclusion that I couldn't do anything for him beyond the occasional visit and support if he needed it, although I didn't think he would ever ask. It had seemed as if we were strangers to each other rather than father and son. I decided I would make a point of calling him now and then, but I doubt if he would ever call me again. I told Jackie later about my visit to Dennis and also told her that I was planning to go to see Gloria. She just nodded, to show me that she understood.

24
Gloria

I knew I had to go and see Gloria to make sure that she understood she could not be involved in the children's lives any more. The thought that she could still be hurting children after so many years horrified me and I had no faith that the Social Services would keep her away from them, since they didn't seem to know anything about our family history or seem able to communicate with one another. I didn't want there to even be a risk that she could get access to any of her grandchildren, even for a meeting.

The night after the television documentary was aired with Gloria appearing, albeit in silhouette, she had rung Wayne, saying how surprised she was by the number of neighbours from New Addington who had apparently known what was happening in the house. She must have wondered why they had never said anything to her at the time, not realizing just what a terrifying figure she had been around the estate and how everyone had tried to avoid having anything to do with her. She didn't seem particularly bothered by the accusations that the programme had made about the state the house was always in and about the way in which she beat and terrorized us. Several of the ex-neighbours had said how the house was filthy, the carpets always wet with urine, and one of them remembered watching one of the children peeing on the floor and no one bothering to clear it up.

I hadn't seen Gloria since she came to our wedding and in the film she still looked like a very big, powerful, domineering woman. I wasn't sure how much of that impression had been created by the camera angles and how much by my own memories of being a small child in her power. To me I guess she will always be a monster, no matter how frail she grows with age.

I'd known that I was going to have to confront her for some months, but I hadn't told anyone of my intention until I told Jackie, because as long as no one else knew, I could wait for the right time to go and face her.

I didn't want to do it on my own and so I decided I wanted to go with Wayne, her favourite son. I asked him to come with me. I wanted there to be someone else around while I talked to her, so that she knew it wasn't just me saying these things. I wanted someone to be a witness to what I was saying and to any response she might have, so she couldn't deny the conversation later. Wayne had been in touch with her over the years and still saw her occasionally. He had some of his stuff stored at her flat, which he wanted to collect so there was a reason for the visit, which would make it seem more natural.

I eventually told him that I wanted to go and see her. 'Why?' he asked.

'I just need to see her about something,' I replied vaguely.

The reason I didn't tell him was that I didn't want Gloria to have any prior warning as to why I was coming so that she would be ready with her arguments and demands. It wasn't that I didn't trust Wayne, it was just that if Gloria asked him what I wanted and he honestly didn't know then there would be no need for him to lie to her. He agreed to come. We made a date for a Wednesday and I said I would pick him up from work in the afternoon and we would drive straight to her flat.

As usual I lay awake the night before, thinking about what I was going to have to say and do the next day. I didn't feel as scared of her now because in my thoughts I was able to control her and put away my memories of what she had done to me for so many years. When I woke up the next morning, after having slept only fitfully I felt deeply lethargic. I got up, but I couldn't put my mind to doing anything. I just went over and over in my mind what I was planning to say to her but none of it sounded quite right. In the end I had to admit to myself that I just didn't feel up to seeing her. It didn't feel right. I didn't want to stumble over my words when I saw her. I wanted to feel confident and strong and not be vindictive. I just felt it was important to make her realize the seriousness of what she was doing to her grand-children. I rang Wayne and postponed our plans until the Friday.

When Friday came I still didn't feel that I was ready to do it. Fortunately Wayne rang and asked if we could put it off again, as he wanted to go out after work with his friends. I agreed readily and we decided to go up to see her on Sunday morning, which was going to be 29 February, a leap year day.

I was beginning to get annoyed with myself, because I knew I was putting off the inevitable and that if I just bit the bullet it would all be over within a few hours. It was like having something left on a 'things to do' list. The longer I put it off the more time I was wasting thinking about it. I knew I just needed to get it over and done with.

I woke up early on the Sunday morning, before anyone else got up, feeling ready to confront her. I didn't even bother to shower, just got dressed. The kids got up shortly afterwards and I gave them their breakfast, all the time feeling more and more confident about what I was planning to do. It was a sunny morning as I set off to pick up Wayne. The roads were empty and I was actually getting a buzz from the idea of going to see her at last and finally getting what I had to say off my chest.

Once we were in the car on our way into London Wayne phoned Gloria on her mobile to tell her we were coming up. I was now feeling eager to get the job done. We chatted as brothers usually do.

'The reason I'm going to see her is to tell her to leave children alone,' I confessed as we drove along. 'Because if she doesn't she's going to end up getting into serious trouble.'

I'd already told Wayne, after we'd met to film the documentary, about Gloria smacking her grandchildren, which had shocked him.

'Why didn't anyone tell me?' he asked.

'I suppose I thought you already knew,' I said.

'I never knew anything about it.'

'I guess she wouldn't do it while you were around.' We left it at that, both ashamed that we couldn't have done more to prevent it.

We parked outside her block of flats and I was quite surprised by how clean it was. I suppose I'd been expecting something more like our old house had been, with rubbish piled up everywhere. Wayne pressed the buzzer for her flat but there was no answer. He pressed again and nothing. My heart sank. Just as I'd got my courage up to confront her she'd chickened out and done a runner.

Wayne called her mobile phone again.

'It's OK,' he said as he hung up. 'She was just going to go to the paper shop but she's coming now.'

We walked back to the car to wait for her. A few minutes later she appeared round the corner. She had cheap, bleached blonde hair, almost white but stained with cigarette smoke. She was wearing a pair of trousers and a jumper, her bare feet pushed into her slippers despite the chill February air. She noticed us as we got out the car and we headed towards her, Wayne leading the way and me following on behind. As we walked towards her I realized she was still a big woman, that wasn't a trick of my memory. She was at least as tall as me, possibly taller, but apart from that she just looked like any other old lady. That idea shocked me. I'd expected her to be different in some way, still the ogre of my memory.

'All right?' was all she said by way of a greeting before she started talking about herself, just rattling on as we walked towards the flats together. She saw me, but didn't make any expression or gesture and just carried on as if I wasn't there. I didn't say anything. The last thing she had said to me was that she was going to kill herself and I had replied, 'Why don't you?'

Still talking, she opened the door to the block to let us into the hallway, which smelled strongly of disinfectant. That took me by surprise. I'd been expecting to be greeted by the same stale smells of neglect and dirt that I remembered from my childhood. One window had been broken, but otherwise there was no damage.

'That's where they meet sometimes.' She gestured to some chairs set out at the end of the hall. 'I don't go down that end. I don't get on with some of the others.'

She wasn't exactly communicating with us, more chatting on to cover what might have been an awkward silence. As she let us into her ground-floor flat she talked on about the doorbell and security systems, a steady stream of words that I wasn't really listening to as I gathered my thoughts about what I was going to say to her once we were inside the flat.

As she let us in through her front door I couldn't believe my eyes, or any of my other senses. Not only was it clean and tidy, there were even homely touches like a carpet on the floor, fresh fruit in a bowl on the coffee table and a frozen turkey dinner defrosting on the side in the kitchen. The little kitchen table was laid up with cutlery in preparation for her meal. The place bore no resemblance to the hellhole we'd been forced to live in as children. Here everything was orderly and controlled and civilized. She was still babbling on, showing us the cord that she could pull on in an emergency and someone would come to her assistance if she ever got into trouble. As she talked my eyes were still looking around in wonder. I noticed a large doll standing on the other side of the room beside the sideboard. Its arms were pulled up and its hands were covering its eyes, which seemed appropriate. There was none of the dirty, stale smell that I had expected and which would have reminded me of childhood. Without children, it seemed, she could cope with life. I remembered how, in the documentary, she had said that if she could change anything in her life it would have been the number of children she had, that she would have stopped at two and not six. My sisters, not surprisingly, were very hurt by the comment, but it did suggest that Gloria realized her own limitations and knew why things had gone so badly wrong. She liked cute little things, like the doll or the teddies that surrounded the sideboard, and real things like babies and puppies, just like a child would. But as soon as they got under her feet she would be unable to cope and would turn on them in a rage so fierce that it was hard to comprehend unless you'd actually seen it. It was like asking a child to look after a family when all it wanted was a teddy bear to play with or a baby for a couple of hours a day when it was joyful and undemanding. But whether it was babies or puppies, anything that spent time with her always ended up cringing in the corners of a room, terrified of receiving another beating. Child or animal it made no difference to her.

As my eyes continued to scan the lounge I noticed that there were five picture frames hanging on the wall, four of which were photos that Jackie had sent her of our wedding. The first was of Jackie and me in our wedding outfits, with Gloria standing next to us in the clothes we had bought for her. The next was of me, Wayne and Jackie, the next of Jackie and me cutting the cake and then a group photo. In the final frame was a collage of different pictures of her grandchildren, including our daughter. I was amazed as I looked around, trying to take it all in as she waffled on.

In the middle of the room on top of a coffee table stood a bowl of fresh fruit and next to it was a little wicker basket, lined with tin foil to keep it clean. Inside were a few pick-and-mix sweets.

'I bet these were full the other day,' I said, completely unable to think of anything else to say.

'Yeah. Have one if you want,' she said, still keeping her eyes away from me.

Wayne disappeared off to get his stuff from a cupboard somewhere and Gloria rolled herself a cigarette while I stayed standing. She did it with a deftness born of long experience. When the operation was complete she stood up and went to the back door, opening it to let the smoke out. Then she sat back down and lit up, pulling a clean ashtray within reach. I couldn't believe my eyes. Never in my life could I remember her opening a door or a window to allow fresh air into our house. There had never been any respite from the smells and the filth when I lived with her.

The fresh cold air drifted into the tidy little flat, carrying the smoke away and she continued talking as if she had done nothing unusual, as if this was how she had always behaved. I couldn't believe I was talking to the same woman who had made my life and everyone else's in the family such hell. Could this seemingly normal old lady really have been the monster of my memory? Wayne had once told me that she was different from how we remembered, but I hadn't been able to believe him.

Then it occurred to me that she could only live like this without the pressure of children. If she got any sort of access to her grandchildren she would instantly revert to her former self, as she must have done on the night that she had attacked my sister's children. With these thoughts I suddenly remembered why I was there and felt my resolve returning.

'I've got to tell you something,' I said. She still didn't look at me. 'You have to leave children alone. You can't go anywhere near them. Do you understand?'

She nodded. She didn't protest or argue or question what I was saying or look as if she didn't know what I was talking about. I looked at her, but she couldn't look back. She just nodded. She knew exactly what I was talking about. Her eyes were staring at the floor as she took another long slow drag of her roll-up.

The next moment she stood up and I moved out of her way as she continued talking as if I'd said nothing. Wayne came back into the room asking for a bin bag to put his things in. She got him a bag and he continued to pack.

'Can you sit down,' I said, unsure if she had taken in what I was saying to her, 'because you really have to understand what I'm saying to you.' My voice sounded anxious but controlled.

She had already finished her cigarette by this time and was rolling herself another one as she sat down.

'Do you understand what I'm telling you? If you do not leave children alone you are going to get into serious, serious trouble. Do you understand?'

She nodded again.

'Do you know what I would do, if I was you?' I went on. 'I would enjoy the rest of your life without children. I wouldn't bother to even try to go near your grand-children, especially the ones who have been taken into care. We both know what goes on. You have to leave them alone. Do you understand?'

'Yes,' she said, her voice subdued, as if she was a child being told off.

As she sat there with me standing over her I began to wonder if I was being a bully, but the thought quickly went out of my mind when the memories of what she had done to her grandchildren returned. I was just saying it as it was. I really wanted to drive home how serious the situation had become. Wayne heard me and glanced at Gloria. I saw her look at him as he continued to pack his things. Now I'd said what I'd come there for I wanted to go as quickly as possible. Wayne finished packing and we went to leave.

In the hall I repeated my message one more time.

'Do you understand, you have to leave children alone?'

She nodded again, still not making any eye contact.

'I hope for your sake you do, because I am deadly serious.'

She came outside with us, wanting to go to the news-agent as she had intended when we arrived. She was talking again and her voice had become loud, just like I remembered it, perhaps because I had made her nervous. She walked off towards the shop without a goodbye or even a backward glance. As she disappeared around the corner I looked up at the bright winter sun and smiled with relief.

'Fuck me,' I said as we made our way back to the car.

'I told you,' Wayne said. 'It's not the same now.'

'So why does she still do this stuff to the kids?'

He shrugged. 'I don't know. Had I known I would have done something about it.'

As I drove home I found myself looking at people walking past; normal-looking old ladies like Gloria, and tired-looking old men like Dennis, and I wondered what went on behind their closed doors. How did they cope with the pressures of life? Were they violent and unable to control their tempers? How many of them, like Gloria, had been beaten as children and so knew no better than to do it to their own families? If there are no records of what she did, how many others are there who the Social Services know nothing about, who go unchecked until it's too late and more damage is done?

I felt relieved that I had finally managed to face her. There was no love between us, but I had known that before I even got there. I'd never treated her like a mother and she'd never treated me like a son. I'd realized that she wanted to get back into our lives, but now that she knew I could remember everything she did to me through those long years, there was no way we could be anything to each other except strangers, only knowing each other through what we read. Wayne and

Gloria

I made little conversation as I took him home, both of us deep in thoughts that we didn't want to share with each other. After dropping Wayne off I felt a real weight lift off my shoulders. I became excited about my life once again because I knew how to deal with my past at last. I had finally put it all behind me. As I walked into the house I gave my children a huge hug and shot Jackie a loving smile.

25

The Next Move

Shortly after going to see Gloria and Dennis I finally met Carol face to face and the social worker now in charge of some of the children. We discussed my sister's children and she told me how they were coming on in leaps and bounds now that they were settled. I said I thought they had been dealt with in a disgusting manner and the social worker agreed, but then went to great lengths to explain that now they were in the system they were finally protected. Three of them were being suggested for adoption and the two older ones for long-term fostering.

Her words made me think hard about what had happened over the past eighteen months or so. It seems to me from my own experience, the experience of my nephews and nieces and from the letters I receive, that the more vulnerable a person is, whether it be a child, a disabled person or an old-age pensioner, the harder it is to have their abusers convicted of their crimes.

The most potentially vulnerable members of our society, therefore, are the least protected. It's easy to blame Social Services or others in authority when things go wrong, but in most cases they are good people doing their best. Despite this I believe there are still a number of ways in which we can improve the situation for the future. Firstly, Social Services must have our whole-hearted support in order for them to recruit more dedicated staff, and the government must provide sufficient funds for this. We must all stop being so negative about the service. Social workers who are out in the field dealing with dysfunctional families need to be given every possible bit of help and support and not be stifled by bureaucracy.

Secondly, those who work in Social Services need to take total responsibility for their actions. At the moment when anything does go wrong all they seem to do is squabble over whose fault it was and moan about the pressures of the job.

In the end every case comes down to being the responsibility of one individual. These individuals need to find satisfaction from their jobs and feel fulfilled by them if they are going to be effective, just like in any other line of work. Part of that satisfaction should come from accepting the consequences of their actions. The consequences of people doing a bad job, when vulnerable children are at risk, are too serious to contemplate.

Thirdly, the spread of information seems at best clumsy and uncontrolled, and at worst dangerous. The new children's bill seems to bring different agencies and professionals together to share information, which is a good development and hopefully will be an ongoing process, with the information being continuously updated.

Fourthly, but most importantly, we need to make parents and guardians as responsible for their actions as we do teachers, doctors, nurses, the police, Social Services and other bodies. We put so much pressure on all these agencies to act responsibly towards our children, where the first port of call should be those who have the most access to them, that is the parents and guardians.

In my experience many of the abusers in our society genuinely believe they are doing nothing wrong. Others are aware of their wrongdoing but believe they can get away with it because their victim is too scared or unempowered to report them.

It must be made easier for the abused to report their problem and to feel confident that if they do so there will be someone there to help them. There must be a system whereby it is known by everyone that if you abuse vulnerable people you will be punished. For example, if a man walks into a pub and breaks a bottle over another man's head, he knows the likely consequences are that he will be arrested and charged. If a parent hits a child over the head with a saucepan in a fit of temper, the chances are they have no such expectation of being punished.

As a nation we have to decide what punishment we think that sort of parental abuse should receive, but we are all still very unclear about that unless someone is murdered. Even in child-murder cases a lot of the perpetrators seem to get away with their crimes. Once we have decided what the punishment should be we must inform everyone, for example with advertising campaigns, just as we advertise the consequences of drink-driving at Christmas time. It is never a simple matter because there are so many possible mitigating circumstances, so many factors to be taken into consideration and argued about, but all the time we are debating and arguing children continue to be attacked. Potential abusers must know what the minimum punishment would be for systematically abusing a child.

But the responsibility doesn't end with the authorities. It belongs to all of us. So what can we all do as individuals to help all the children whose childhoods go so terribly wrong? The answer seems to be that we all have to try a little bit harder to help those who need it, be more vigilant and not so willing to turn a blind eye, whether the children are our relatives, our neighbours, our friends or our pupils.

We also need to educate our children as to what it means to be a parent. They must be encouraged to create lives for themselves before they go on to produce families of their own, and to be very sure they can cope before they set out on the difficult path of parenthood. Everyone needs to be made fully aware of the responsibility and pressures involved in bringing up children so that they can decide whether they are up to it. All of us probably know of someone with small children who could do with a little help. We must never be shy of offering it.

Also, more good people need to be encouraged to provide foster care, and more people need to be encouraged to adopt children over the age of three. There is always a shortage of safe homes. If you are interested, pick up the phone or go on to the Internet and research all the fostering and adoption agencies. I know now's not the right time for Jackie and me to foster, but one day I hope we will.

None of these measures is going to be enough on its own and I fear there will always be children who fall through the net, like I did for so many years. But the more each one of us does, the less likely it is to happen to a child we know. We all have to be a little bit more determined to help in a society that mainly helps itself.

As the spring approaches Mistico is now fit and ready to play and I am looking forward to the forthcoming polo season. I have completed my film script and am currently having the storyboards drawn out shot by shot, bringing my dream ever closer. After that has happened I plan to find an agent who will put me in touch with producers and financiers to get my movie funded. It won't be easy, I understand that, but I am as determined as ever and, as always, I'll be knocking on that door until it eventually opens and I can continue to follow my dream.

I have started work on my first novel and am continuing to take my inventions forward, constructing models and ensuring they work, and I am finally going through the process of patenting them. I have set up a charity called the Sunflower Children's Trust which raises money and awareness for smaller, less well-known children's charities and organizations, especially focusing on the inner cities and our most deprived areas.

As you know my family mean everything to me and we all work hard to have a good life together. I look forward to showing them what I can achieve and to giving them security through my efforts. As the children grow up and start to become independent they will make mistakes as we all do, but Jackie and I will always be there to guide them and comfort them and support them, which is the best any parent can ever do.

I've always wanted to prove what I can do; now I have the chance and I'm grabbing it with both hands. Because I no longer want to look back I won't be writing any more about my childhood or the Lewis family.

I have thought a great deal about why so many people want to read a story like mine and I think there may be two reasons. One must be that they have endured some sort of similar experience, or at least know of someone else who has, and the other must be that they are trying to find out what happens in a world that they can't imagine, because their childhoods were as happy as they should have been.

I think it is very encouraging that people want to know what happens in dysfunctional families like the Lewises because it means they are more likely to spot the danger signals when they see them in other families, and to believe children when they say they are being mistreated. If I am right in thinking that many others are reading it because they have had similar experiences, then it seems that we still have a very long way to go as a society before we can truly say that we are civilized in the way we treat our children.

When I reach my twilight years I want to be able to look back and say, 'Well, the start wasn't all that good, but I sure as hell made up for it with the rest.'

I still want the farm I was dreaming of at the end of writing *The Kid*, and I still want to travel America, but instead of trying to achieve my dreams a hundred different ways at once, I am now more focused. I dream of a big open room with its own character and life, filled with the smell of a large open fireplace, where I can spend the days with my creations. The walls will be blank so that I can go back to writing on them, in my own world with my family near me. It will take a lifetime to cover those walls, but they will end up filled with my life.

Finally I must thank all of you for your support; the people working in the media, the bookshops and the supermarkets who drew *The Kid* to everyone's attention and you, the readers, who took the time to buy and read it. It was you and *The Kid* that helped me get on my feet and live my dreams. From the bottom of my heart I thank you all.

K.